Can the Euro be Saved?

The Future of Capitalism series

Published titles
Steve Keen, *Can We Avoid Another Financial Crisis?*
Malcolm Sawyer, *Can the Euro be Saved?*

Malcolm Sawyer

Can the Euro
be Saved?

polity

First published in 2018 by Polity Press

Polity Press
65 Bridge Street
Cambridge CB2 1UR, UK

Polity Press
350 Main Street
Malden, MA 02148, USA

ISBN-13: 978-1-5095-1524-0
ISBN-13: 978-1-5095-1525-7(pb)

A catalogue record for this book is available from the British Library.

Typeset in 11 on 15 Sabon by
Servis Filmsetting Ltd, Stockport, Cheshire
Printed and bound in the UK by Clays Ltd, St Ives PLC

For further information on Polity, visit our website: politybooks.com

Contents

1	The Euro Crises	1
2	The Shaky Foundations of the Euro Project	9
3	The Failures of the Euro Area	44
4	An Agenda for Prosperity	72
5	Barriers to Progress	99
	Notes	123
	References	129

1

The Euro Crises

During the past decade, there has been much talk of the 'euro crisis', with profound economic and financial difficulties besetting the euro area.[1] It would be more appropriate to talk of a set of interrelated crises plaguing the euro area and its citizens. There is an existential crisis which still rumbles on with the question of whether a fixed exchange-rate system and a monetary union without political union are sustainable. There are strong elements of sovereign debt crises. There are balance-of-payments crises with large underlying current account imbalances between member countries which have been addressed through internal deflation but would become manifest again if there were any significant recoveries in countries such as Portugal and Greece. There is an unemployment crisis, particularly concerning youth unemployment.

The Euro Crises

This book aims to set out the nature of the economic and political problems facing the euro area, which can be put under the heading 'Euro crises', exploring the ways in which the design of the euro area and its policy agenda were faulty from the beginning and how those 'design faults' have stymied the economic prospects of the people in the euro area. It outlines a broad policy agenda which could address those 'design faults', without which it is argued the economies of the euro area will continue to stumble. But the implementation of a policy agenda along the lines suggested is not presently promoted by any significant political forces and would face enormous obstacles.

There is a marked contrast between the first decade of the euro (1998 to 2007) and its second decade (2008 to 2017). The euro was launched as a virtual currency for financial transactions in 1998, with introduction to the public in 2001. By 2001, 12 countries had adopted the euro, which are labelled EU-12 below, and were subsequently joined by a further seven.[2] It was launched with great hopes for potential contributions to economic and political integration within the European Union and stimulating economic growth and employment. Even now (2017), the European Union website can state that:

A single currency offers many advantages, such as eliminating fluctuating exchange rates and exchange costs. Because it is easier for companies to conduct cross-border trade and the economy is more stable, the economy grows and consumers have more choice. A common currency also encourages people to travel and shop in other countries. At global level, the euro gives the EU more clout, as it is the second most important international currency after the US dollar.[3]

Reviewing the first decade, the European Commission was able to claim that:

[w]e have good reason to be proud of our single currency. The Economic and Monetary Union and the euro are a major success. For its member countries, the EMU has anchored macroeconomic stability, and increased cross border trade, financial integration and investment. For the EU as a whole, the euro is a keystone of further economic integration and a potent symbol of our growing political unity. And for the world, the euro is a major new pillar in the international monetary system and a pole of stability for the global economy. (Joaquín Almunia 2008, then Commissioner for Economic and Monetary Affairs in European Economy)

Despite the optimism expressed by the European Commission (EC), the economic performance of the euro area in the first decade of the euro could be described as lacklustre. The economies of the member states grew, but not as quickly as comparable countries nor as quickly as hitherto.[4] The EU-12 had an average growth rate over the period 2002 to 2008 of 1.7% per annum, with Germany at 1.3%, France 1.8% and Italy 0.9%. Unemployment had tended to decline, though the average rate over 2002 to 2008 was 8.1% with a rate of 7.6% in 2007. The European Commission (2008: 6), among others, claimed that 'the bulk of these improvements reflect reforms of both labour markets and social security systems carried out under the Lisbon Strategy for Growth and Jobs and the coordination and surveillance framework of the European Monetary Union (EMU), as well as the wage moderation that has characterised most euro area countries.' The promised boom in trade between the euro countries did not materialize.[5] By the mid-2000s, signs were already there of problems arising. There were differences in inflation, and more significantly the current account imbalances between the EU-12 were widening.

The second decade of the euro has been a 'lost decade' of slow and often negative growth and high unemployment. Further, 'while already it is clear that Europe is facing a lost decade, there is a risk that in a few years' time we will be speaking of Europe's lost quarter of a century' (Stiglitz 2016). The second decade of the euro has been dominated by the financial crisis and its aftermath, a widespread recession and firefighting sovereign debt and banking crises.

A central theme of this book is that the euro area suffers from major 'design faults', and so resolving the economic malaise of the euro area will require a massive redesign: I develop some ideas for this in chapter 4. I would echo the sentiments of de Grauwe when he wrote that:

> The Eurozone looked like a wonderful construction at the time it was built. Yet it appeared to be loaded with design failures. In 1999 I compared the Eurozone to a beautiful villa in which Europeans were ready to enter. Yet it was a villa that did not have a roof. As long as the weather was fine, we would like to have settled in the villa. We would regret it when the weather turned ugly. With the benefit of hindsight, the design failures have become even more manifest as the ones that were perceived before the start. (De Grauwe 2013: 1)

The caveat is that for some of us the eurozone never looked like a wonderful construction (Arestis and Sawyer 1996).[6] As de Grauwe (2015) notes from the start, some economists (albeit a minority) 'warned that ... design failures would lead to problems and conflicts within the currency union, and that the Eurozone in the end would fall apart if these failures were not corrected'.

The 'design faults' have been present through the existence of the euro, though they were brought into sharp relief by the financial crisis and recession. Some of the 'design faults' were presaged by the convergence criteria for membership of the euro dating from the Maastricht Treaty of 1992. In those criteria, emphasis was placed on limits on budget deficits and public debt, on inflation (but not on inflationary conditions), and on stability of the exchange rate, but not on whether the exchange rate was at an appropriate level; nor was any attention given to the current account positions and their sustainability. These 'design faults' were intensified by the adoption of the Stability and Growth Pact, and the nature of the relationship of the European Central Bank with national governments and with the financial sector, and its reluctance to act as a lender of last resort. These 'design faults' were significant factors in the relatively poor performance of countries forming the eurozone, even before the financial crisis, and intensified the effects of that crisis and constrained the policy responses. The policies of the euro area are locked into an austerity agenda with the requirements to drive a balanced budget, no matter what the economic circumstances of the country concerned, including its requirements for public investment in infrastructure.

There are still, and will long remain, considerable diversities between the member countries in terms of their economic circumstances and political and institutional arrangements, which have not been significantly reduced by the experience of a single currency. The present EMU policies make a return to prosperity very difficult, and the future for euro-area prosperity appears bleak. The euro itself will likely continue, though the membership of the euro area may diminish. However, it will be argued that, with the present policy arrangements, there will not be prosperity across all members of the euro area.

There is a need for fundamental reforms within the EMU to secure future prosperity across the union. The reforms which are required for a prosperous EMU are outlined. The present policies can be described as ordo-liberal – combining neo-liberal macroeconomic policies with the constitutional embedding of those policies. This is exemplified by the 'fiscal compact', which not only lays down the requirement for a balanced structural budget but also embeds those requirements in national constitutions. The types of reform which are required could be labelled those of 'more Europe', and as such will meet intense political obstacles when the political climate appears hostile to such developments. The policy changes, particularly with respect to fiscal and monetary policies, challenge the dominant ordo-liberal agenda of the euro area.

The attention throughout this book is on economic policies within the euro area and on alternative policies which address the euro crises. There is another important agenda which has to be simultaneously addressed – that is, the democratic deficit within the European Union. Such an agenda should consider giving more power to the European Parliament in economic (and other) decision making; fiscal policies under the democratic control of national parliaments; and ending the independence of the European Central Bank.

2

The Shaky Foundations of the Euro Project

Introduction

Ideas for a single currency for (some or all of) the members of the European Union can be traced back to at least 1970 with the Werner Report (1970), which advocated movement towards economic and monetary union with completion by 1980. It proposed reaching monetary union in three stages, an idea repeated in the later Delors Report (Committee for the Study of Economic and Monetary Union 1989).[1] There was a clear view that '[a] monetary union implies inside its boundaries the total and irreversible convertibility of currencies, the elimination of margins of fluctuation in exchange rates, the irrevocable fixing of parity rates and the complete liberation of movements of capital' (Werner Report 1970: 5). The Marjolin Report (1975) argued that monetary union should be postponed until after the achievement of a high degree of economic integration in the European Union. It advocated that a single unified market would provide a sound basis from which to launch monetary union, and this found its expression in the 'single market' achieved in 1992. The MacDougall Report (European Commission 1977) stressed the role of a unified fiscal system in a monetary union and concluded that a monetary union would not be viable without a sufficiently large community budget for fiscal policy which estimated an amount of 7.5 per cent of EU GDP (as compared with an EU budget currently around 1 per cent of GDP). Although many had argued for the importance of a fiscal union alongside the single currency, these arguments made no impact on the policy formation of the euro.

The more concrete developments of a single currency started with the Maastricht Treaty (formally the Treaty on European Union), signed in February 1992, which set the framework for the moves towards the establishment of a single currency. The establishment of the 'single market' in 1992 had represented a major step in the process of market integration, along with the removal of non-tariff barriers to trade between EU member states, resulting from the harmonization of product standards and so on, and a reduction of cross-border checks on trade. The single currency could be seen as the next step in economic integration by removing exchange rate risks, transactions costs and so forth between the member states that adopted it.

Convergence criteria and membership of the euro area

The Maastricht Treaty established the criteria to be applied to a country's membership of the euro area, whereby a member country of the EU meeting the criteria had to accept membership (a requirement from which Denmark and the United Kingdom secured an opt-out) and those criteria had to be met before a country could become a member. It is a matter of debate as to how far those criteria were set in the expectation that a number of countries could not meet them, and thereby would be excluded from membership of the eurozone, at least in the first round. However, in the event, during the decision as to who would be the initial members of the euro area, the application of the convergence criteria was fudged,[2] and indeed all 12 countries out of all then 15 member states who wished to join were able to do so.

The convergence criteria to be applied to a country for adoption of the euro, and which continue to apply for potential new members, are:

1   The country's exchange rate is not to deviate by more than 2.25% from its central rate for the two years prior to membership, and hence there is a degree of stability before the locking of the currency into the euro;

2   A country's inflation rate is not to exceed the average rate of inflation of the three community nations with the lowest inflation rate by 1.5%, reflecting the need for broadly comparable inflation rates between the constituent parts of a currency union;

3   A country's long-term interest rates are not to exceed the average interest rate of the three countries with the lowest inflation rate by 2%, as a single policy interest rate applies across a currency union;

4   The government budget deficit is not to exceed 3% of its GDP, a foretaste of the concerns over budget deficits;

5   Overall government debt is not to exceed 60% of its GDP.

Countries are also required to have an 'independent central bank', that is, a central bank with operational independence from the national government.

Many considerations were omitted from the convergence criteria, and their omission indicates what was regarded as relevant and significant and what was not. It was those omissions which were the sources of many of the difficulties that have since emerged. There was no mention of convergence of the business cycle that was significant in relation to euro-area macroeconomic policy, which was in effect monetary policy operated by the European Central Bank (ECB). Monetary policy is of necessity an undifferentiated policy and inevitably runs into a 'one size fits all' problem, and convergence of macroeconomic conditions between member countries would ease the problems this has caused. Monetary policy has to be uniform across a currency union, yet the economic issues and problems, which are being addressed by monetary policy, vary across the currency union, that is, in the euro area, by country and by region. The severity of the 'one size fits all' problem is much reduced if the conditions in the member regions are closely correlated (e.g. the movements of output, inflation) and if the responses of economic variables of relevance to the policy instruments (e.g. interest rates) are similar between member regions.

There was no recognition of the differences in living standards between countries. There was also a lack of concern over the level of unemployment, with no reference to low levels of unemployment being an objective of monetary policy (or any other policy). And no account was taken of the differences between countries over unemployment on entry into a fixed exchange-rate regime. Yet there were large differences in unemployment rates between member countries (which largely continue). In 2000, unemployment rates varied from 2.2% (Luxembourg), 3.9% (Austria) through to 11.2% (Greece), 11.9% (Spain); by 2015, Greece (24.9%) and Spain (22.1%) remained the countries with the highest rates of unemployment, though by now Germany had become the country with lowest unemployment, at 4.6%, with Austria and Luxembourg at 5.7% and 6.5% respectively. Consideration of further unemployment in the regions (of member countries) reveals much larger differences – ranging in 2015 from a number of regions with unemployment rates below 5% to regions with unemployment rates up to 30%. This constrains high-unemployment countries in their ability to draw level with fellow euro-area member countries with relatively low unemployment. A country with high unemployment would have to find additional sources of demand for its output if its unemployment record is to improve, and to do so without a serious deterioration in its current account position.

The convergence criteria required convergence of inflation rates at the time of admission into the EMU, but it only applies at a point in time. It is well known that the constituent members of the EMU had previously experienced substantially different inflation patterns: for example, during the 1980s Germany had an average annual inflation rate of 2.6%, while Italy experienced an average inflation rate of 10% and Greece 19%; figures for the 1990s were 2.5%, 4.2% and 11.1% respectively, with many countries on a downward trend of inflation as they strove to meet the inflation requirements for membership of the single currency. But there was little concern in the convergence criteria as to whether there were similarities in the inflationary processes and experiences between countries. Thus, whether there was a tendency for any country to inflate faster than another or whether inflationary expectations were similar was ignored, despite the marked differences in inflation experience in the preceding decades. There was also no regard paid to differences in the inflationary barriers between countries, that is, differences in the unemployment

rate which may be consistent with constant inflation. The creation of the single currency may have
generated some conditions which would be conducive to less divergence in inflation experience (e.g.
trade between countries in a common currency
placing pressure on prices). But crucially there
was no criterion on inflationary conditions being
similar. This includes any underlying trends in the
rates of inflation, the wage and price determination
mechanisms, the responsiveness of domestic prices
to foreign price changes and the effects of fluctuations in demand and economic activity on wage and
price inflation.

Persistent differences in the rates of inflation
amongst member countries of a fixed exchange-rate
regime (and a currency union is such a regime) will
eventually prove to be unsustainable. Prices and
costs in countries experiencing relatively high inflation will rise in comparison with prices and costs in
countries experiencing relatively low inflation. The
goods and services produced in the high-inflation
countries tend to become uncompetitive in comparison with those produced in low-inflation countries.
The average rise in prices for each country over the
period 1998 to 2008 outlined in Figure 2.1 gives
some impression of the differences between the
euro-area founder member countries. Countries

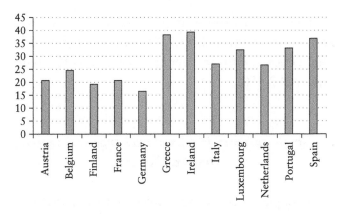

Figure 2.1 Price rises in euro-area countries, 1998–2008 (%)

Source: Calculated from OECD *Economic Outlook*, various issues

often experienced inflation above the 2% target level, albeit usually by less than 1 percentage point. The (unweighted) average rate for the 12 countries was 2–3% every year from 2000 to 2008. In the decade from 1998, the cumulative price rises varied from 16.4% in Germany through to 38% and 39% in Greece and Ireland respectively. Thus there were significant shifts in relative prices between countries. The statistics in Figure 2.1 refer to consumer prices (which is the target for monetary policy). Also of significance for international trade is the development of measures of competitiveness and prices of tradeable goods. Over the period 2000–2009, the annual average rise in unit labour costs was 0.6% for Germany through to 3.9% for Ireland and 4.5% for Greece, with an average (across the 12 countries) of 2.4%.

A single currency is a fixed exchange-rate regime par excellence

The single currency was welcomed by many as a further step to economic integration, and most EU member countries were keen to adopt the euro. The single currency was viewed as encouraging trade through the removal of exchange rate risk and of transactions costs, which would boost growth and lower interest rates for most countries so that they would converge with the level of interest rates in Germany and lower inflation. The fixed exchange rate involved in a single currency would help to constrain inflation rates and lock them onto the low German inflation rate. Lower inflation and interest rates were indeed realized, though the anticipated boosts to trade and growth were generally not achieved. The single currency, along with the removal of remaining capital controls, encouraged the movement of capital between member countries. There was indeed increased capital mobility, but in turn this was a contributory factor to the development of credit booms and asset price inflation which played a significant role in the financial crisis.

A single currency locks together the constituent currencies in perpetuity. For example, the value of the Deutschmark entered at 1.95583 DM per euro (and the calculations are made to six significant figures), the French franc at 6.55957 FF per euro, and the Italian lira at 1936.27, and hence the cross-exchange rates at 1 DM = 3.353386 FF = 990 lira; and similarly for all of the other constituent currencies. In the decade before the locking together, the exchange rate between Deutschmark and French franc had been rather stable, whereas the exchange rate between the Deutschmark and the Italian lira had moved from 1 DM = 741 lira (1988) to 1137 lira (1995) before falling back.

When each country has its own currency, the exchange rates between the currencies can and do vary. The frequency of changes in the exchange rate of a currency can, of course, vary, from second to second, when a floating exchange rate is set by the exchange markets, to infrequently, when fixed exchange rates are decided by the governments concerned. It is, however, highly relevant that adjustments to the nominal exchange rate are possible, a possibility that is removed by the adoption of a single currency. The first significance of this concerns the inflation rate: under a single currency with the ultra-fixed exchange rate between countries, the inflation rates in the constituent countries have to be broadly in line. The relationship between exchange rate and inflation illustrates this: differences in the inflation rate between countries may be met by a depreciation of the exchange rate of the country having the higher rate of inflation. On the other hand, without that option of an exchange rate adjustment, the inflation rates in the two countries would need to be aligned; countries prone to higher inflation are pushed to adopting deflationary policies to constrain their rate of inflation (in line with other member countries).

When a country has its own currency, there is at least the possibility that it can change its exchange rate. In response to a downturn in economic fortunes, it can devalue its currency, thereby stimulating the demand for its production. In response to a rate of inflation above that of its trading partners, with the prices of its goods and services rising relative to those of its partners, then its currency can depreciate to offset that. This is not to underestimate the difficulties of nominal exchange rate adjustment. It is rather to highlight that the adoption of a single currency clearly removes the possibility of such an adjustment since the nominal exchange rates between members of the currency union cannot be changed, and other adjustment processes will be required.

In the 'optimal currency area' literature,[3] the question was raised as to what conditions should be in place before a common currency area is formed. It has long been recognized that this fixed exchange rate (between nations) aspect of a currency union removes the flexibility of exchange rate adjustments in the face of what are termed 'asymmetric shocks' – that is, changes in economic conditions which affect one country of the currency union but not others. It could be a favourable 'shock', such as the discovery of natural resources, or an unfavourable shock, such as a downturn in the demand for products in which it specializes. During the formation of the EMU, there was very little attention paid to such considerations and how the euro area could respond to 'asymmetric shocks'. Within that literature, three types of condition were highlighted. First was the idea of relative price flexibility: for example, if the prospects of a country improved (say, through discovery of natural resources or through improvement in the quality of the goods it produced), then prices in that country would rise (relative to prices in other countries). In effect, this could mimic what could happen with separate currencies in that the exchange rate of the currency of a prospering country would rise. In either case, the real exchange rate of the country would rise – in one case through its prices rising, in the other through its nominal exchange rate rising. Within the euro area, prices in one country do vary relative to those in another, which has shown up in terms of differences in the rates of inflation between countries. But those differences are reflections of differences in the institutional arrangements for price and wage determination, rather than of appropriate adjustments in the real exchange rates of the member countries.

A second condition was that of factor mobility between countries – and in particular the mobility of labour moving from those countries suffering an economic downturn to those experiencing an economic boom. It is well known that effective labour mobility with the EU remains low, especially by comparison with the United States. Labour mobility is, however, viewed in terms of an adjustment process which comes with substantial costs, such as the departure of skilled labour from areas suffering from economic downturn. And at most it only addresses asymmetric shocks.

The third condition was the use of fiscal transfers. The level of demand in the economic area in question would to some degree be sheltered from the full effects of the downturn through fiscal transfers. In a nation-state, there is some automatic element in these fiscal transfers – tax revenues to the central government are reduced as a consequence of the lower level of income, and some social security benefits (notably unemployment benefits) are increased. There would often be deliberate responses by the central government in the form of increased assistance of various forms to the economic area. Within a currency area without a central government (as in the case of the euro area), there would not be these fiscal transfers, nor the stabilizing role which they could play.

The entry of countries into a currency union locks together (as illustrated above) the exchange rates between the member countries. It should have been important to ensure that the exchange rates at which the national currencies entered the euro were appropriate and that the pattern of exchange rates was consistent with a sustainable balance-of-payments position. Yet there was little (or no) attention paid to the appropriateness of the exchange rates at which the national currencies entered. The convergence criteria did involve a degree of stability of exchange rate in the two years prior to membership, with the presumption that such stability indicated an appropriate exchange rate. But that element of stability of the nominal exchange rate does not ensure the sustainability of that exchange rate and, more significantly, it does not ensure the sustainability of the balance-of-payments position and current account and capital account imbalances.

A country with a current account deficit (coming from imports exceeding exports and from net outward flow of income) has to borrow from overseas, and sustaining such a deficit requires that such borrowing continues. Yet, as the borrowing continues, the interest and other payments on borrowing mount, and the current account deficit tends to widen. A country having joined a single currency cannot now devalue its currency in an attempt to correct the current account deficit through making exports more attractive and imports more expensive.

When inflationary conditions and the average rate of inflation differ between member countries of a currency union, then prices in the high-inflation countries rise relative to those in the low-inflation countries. The high-inflation countries tend to become uncompetitive relative to the low-inflation ones. There is a limit to how long the differences in inflation can persist without the current account position becoming unsustainable as exports decline and imports increase in the high-inflation countries. Yet the euro area had no policies in place to ensure similarity of inflation conditions.

The mixture of the dissimilarities of inflationary conditions and the lack of consideration of the sustainability of the current account position on entry has now come to haunt the EMU.

The euro as a political project

The euro project can be viewed in terms of its economic impacts, and that is the focus of attention in this book. However, there has always been a close association between money, its creation and role, and the nation-state, and the 'one money-one nation' rule has been in near-universal use. The nation-state has been instrumental in establishing the currency as the unit of account and for determining what will be accepted by the state in payment of taxes and the discharge of debts. The central bank operates as the bank of the state as well as the bank of banks. The central bank is the issuer of currency and provides finance for the central government. The central bank generally operates as a 'lender of last resort' in the sense of proving liquidity to the banking system as and when required and in lending to government and directly or indirectly purchasing government bonds.

Godley (1992) pointed out that 'the establishment of a single currency in the EC would indeed bring to an end the sovereignty of its component nations and their power to take independent actions on major issues. ... [T]he power to issue its own money, to make drafts on its own central bank, is the main thing which defined national independence' (p. 3).

The establishment of the single currency (euro) was clearly viewed as a further step towards integration and the development of an 'ever closer union'. The control of the currency was ceded to a supra-national body in the form of the European Central Bank (ECB), which became responsible for setting the policy interest rate applicable across the whole of the currency union. This intensifies the 'one size fits all' problem of central banking – a single interest rate has to be set that applies across diverse economic regions, and the interest rate suitable for one region that may not be suitable for others in different economic circumstances. Yet, while in the Maastricht programme the establishment and objectives of an independent central bank were set out, there was no mention of central fiscal policy. 'Yet there would simply have to be a system of institutions which fulfils all those functions at a Community level which are at present exercised by the central governments of individual member countries' (Godley 1992: 3).

The relationship between money and the state leads into the question as to whether a currency union requires a political union for its long-term survival. Monetary unions,[4] such as that between England and Scotland (1707) and those of unified Italy (1861), and Germany (1870s), which were linked with political union, have survived long term. Examples of monetary union without political union are limited and include the Belgium–Luxembourg union (from 1923), subsequently absorbed into the euro, the West and Central African CFA franc zone (1948) and the Eastern Caribbean Currency Union (from 1983), which are still in operation. Monetary unions which collapsed when political union collapsed include the Roman monetary union (286 to 301) and, more recently, those of the Soviet Union, Yugoslavia and Czechoslovakia (and, with a long delay, the United Kingdom and Ireland). Temporary monetary unions, such as the Latin monetary union (1865 to 1926) and the Scandinavian currency union (1873 to 1921), and currency pegs, notably the gold standard (1870 to 1931/6) and the Bretton

Woods systems (1944–1973), also proved to be unsustainable.

The single currency is also deeply political in the sense that it reflects the relationships of the member states. The political dimensions cannot, of course, be ignored. Marsh (2013), for example, argues that 'the euro is an overtly political project' (p. 11), though it was largely sold to the public as bringing economic benefits and the completion of the single market. In this regard, much focus has been on the power relationships between Germany and the other member states. As Marsh (2011) argues, 'the creation of the Euro was . . . as much or more a matter of political vision as of economic necessity.' There were 'the strongly aligned efforts of German and French political leaders, supported by central bankers, to bind Europe together with strong political and economic ties'. Marsh (2011) argues that the founders of the euro realized that a political union of some form would be necessary, and many commentators before and since the formation of the euro have stressed the links between currency union and political union.[5] Marsh (2011) for example indicates four major factors for the creation of the euro: to promote growth and employment by elimination of exchange rate risks boosting trade; to complete Franco-German rapprochement by establishing a path towards political union; to create a rival to the dollar as the dominant global currency; and, through a more integrated European community, to constrain the enhanced dominance of a newly united Germany, with a substantial increase in its population and economic size.

A currency union has to have an economic governance structure, notably a supra-national central bank, relationships between that central bank and the member states of the currency union, and a policy agenda towards fiscal policies. Countries come to a currency union with different policy histories and institutional arrangements, and it is inevitable that the policy agendas and governance structures adopted by the currency union area are closer to those previously experienced by some member states than by others. The policy agendas adopted will be more in line with the economic interests of some members of the currency union than others. In the case of the euro area (as will be further discussed in chapter 5), the policy perspectives of Germany had a much greater influence on the area's economic governance structures – the creation of an 'independent' European Central Bank modelled on the German Bundesbank is a clear illustration.

The lack of attention of the political class to the design of the euro and the build-up of pressures along the lines which many commentators had identified from the mid-1990s lies at the heart of many of the problems of the euro area.

Fiscal policies in the EMU

The Stability and Growth Pact (SGP) continued its significant role in limiting the scale of budget deficits and government debt which made their appearance in the Maastricht convergence criteria. The key features of the SGP are that member countries should maintain budget deficits at less than 3% of GDP (with minor exceptions for severe recession). Further, 'member States commit themselves to respect the medium-term budgetary objective of positions close to balance or in surplus set out in their stability of convergence.'[6] Government debt should be maintained at less than 60% of GDP. Figure 2.2 first illustrates the fluctuations in the average budget deficit in the euro area in the decade to 2008. It can be readily seen that after 2000 the average budget was in deficit each year and did not meet the requirements of the SGP. In the second part of Figure 2.2, the average deficit is given by country

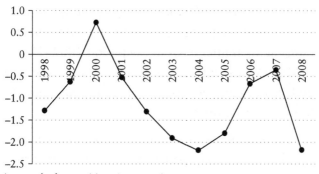

Average budget positions (euro area)

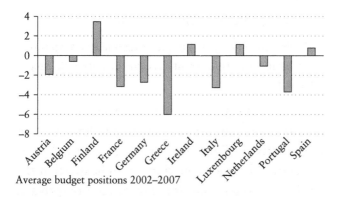

Average budget positions 2002–2007

Figure 2.2 Budget deficits in the euro area (% of GDP)
Source: Calculated from OECD *Economic Outlook,* various issues

for the period 2002 to 2007, where again the ways in which the SGP budget deficit limits were not met are evident. The 3% limit has been breached on many occasions – using figures from the OECD's

31

Economic Outlook, there were 25 times (out of 72 observations) when a country exceeded the 3% limit on an annual basis in the period 2002–2007.

Many of the difficulties encountered by the SGP and more generally can be investigated from the following relationship:

(1) (Private Savings – Private Investment) + (Imports – Exports – Net income from abroad) (current account deficit) + (Tax Revenue minus Government Expenditure) = zero

This can be alternatively expressed:

(2) Private Savings – Private Investment + Capital-Account Surplus (current account deficit) = Budget Deficit

As these stand, they are national income accounts identities and say nothing about the level of economic activity. Equation (1) can be referred to as the sectoral balance equation – it indicates that the net flows into and out of the three sectors (private, foreign, public) have to sum to zero. For example, if tax revenue exceeds government expenditure, there is a net flow of funds into the public sector; and if tax revenue is less than government expenditure, there is a net outflow. Moving from equation (1) to equation (2), there is recognition that a current account deficit has to be funded through an inflow of capital from abroad, that is, the capital-account surplus. The budget deficit is government expenditure minus tax revenue. One interpretation of equation (2) is that the budget deficit is funded through net private savings and inflow of capital.

It needs also to be observed that one country's imports are another country's exports, and the sum of current account positions across all countries is zero – some countries have surpluses and others have deficits. Within the euro area, it was the case during the 2000s that trade with the rest of the world was close to balance and hence the current account position close to zero. This implies that some countries within the euro area had current account surpluses while others had current account deficits. Current account deficits for 1998, 2001 and 2008 are displayed in Figure 2.3. These figures illustrate the sharp differences between euro-area countries in their current account positions and the general tendency for the imbalances between countries to widen over that decade. Those differences in the current account positions and the associated capital-account positions can be seen as a reflection of the export potential of a country and its dependence on imports, and of its ability and need to borrow from abroad.

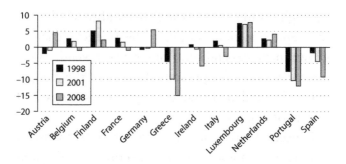

Figure 2.3 Current account positions in the eurozone, 1998–2008 (% GDP)

Source: Calculated from OECD *Economic Outlook,* various issues

Equations (1) and (2) suggest that the budget deficit, net private savings and the current account position are related. It also suggests that a country which has some combination of low or negative net private savings (i.e. investment tending to exceed savings) and of current account surplus (i.e. exports tending to be greater than imports) will find it appropriate to have a budget surplus. Conversely, a country which has some combination of substantial net private savings and current account deficit will find it appropriate to have a budget deficit. As indicated in Figure 2.3, the countries of the euro area have rather different experiences over current account positions. In a similar vein, countries have differing net private savings positions. It is then not surprising the countries differ in their budget positions.

The SGP suffers from two basic and interrelated problems, and these have been intensified in the 'fiscal compact'.

The first set of problems arise from the attempt to impose a 'one size fits all' approach to fiscal policy – to set targets for budget deficit and debt levels to apply across all the member countries, no matter what their history, policy experiences and economic circumstances. The budget position refers to the total budget, including the current and capital budgets. Thus it makes no allowance for the requirements for infrastructure investments in a country. It makes no allowance for different economic circumstances in the country concerned. It can also be seen by reference to equation (1) that a country with a current account surplus (with exports tending to exceed imports) and/or high tendency for investment will find a budget surplus more appropriate than will others. Germany and some other member countries with large export surpluses can more readily achieve a budget surplus.

The second is that the target set is for some form of balanced budget (initially averaged over the cycle, tightened in the 'fiscal compact' to structural budget in balance).[7] It draws on an approach to fiscal policy which is concerned with the size of the budget deficit rather than a fiscal policy (along the lines of 'functional finance') where the policy is used to influence the level of demand in the economy and to pursue objectives including a high level of employment. It assumes that the achievement of a balanced budget is actually feasible in all member countries. Equation (2) above shows that a balanced budget requires that Private Savings – Private Investment + Capital-Account Surplus (current account deficit) = zero. A country with a tendency for savings to exceed investment and/or to run a current account deficit would not be able to readily achieve a balanced budget.[8]

Fiscal transfers

The euro area has been notable for the lack of fiscal transfers between the component national states affected by some federal authority. The role of such transfers would combine a transfer of spending power from the relatively rich area to the relatively poor area and would serve to limit the effects on an area from an asymmetric shock. A federal-level fiscal policy would also serve to operate across the piece as an automatic stabilizer. But a federal fiscal policy would need the ability to run significant budget deficits and not to be constrained by any necessity to balance the budget over some time horizon. The significant advantage of a federal fiscal policy of this type would be that a region particularly hard hit by recession would have received fiscal assistance rather than having to rely on its own borrowing to operate a budget deficit sufficient to contain the worst effects of the recession. The strength of the euro area (or the EMU or the EU) would have permitted necessary borrowing at more conducive interest rates than a country left to itself. The euro area would have the major advantage in this regard in that it would be borrowing in its own currency, and so there would be no risk of default on the debt simply because the euro area (through the European Central Bank) would, albeit indirectly, in effect always be able to create sufficient money to pay any debts. The significant issue for national governments within the EMU is that their borrowing is in effect in a foreign currency in the sense that the euro was a currency where the national government had no control over the volume of the currency.

Many have argued that a monetary union will have to be embedded in a significant fiscal union. This is probably the hardest part of the process to make the eurozone sustainable in the long run, as the willingness to transfer significant spending and taxing powers to European institutions is very limited. It remains a necessary part, though. 'Without significant steps towards fiscal union there is no future for the euro' (De Grauwe 2013: 31).

European Central Bank

The European Central Bank (ECB) was established as an 'independent' institution, where independence means no interference from any other institution or individual at all. The national central banks, which along with the ECB form the European System of Central Banks (ESCB), are also independent. The price stability objective of the ECB is interpreted as inflation below but close to 2%. The independence of the ECB and the objective of price stability fit with the idea of inflation targeting. The ECB failed to meet the price stability target of inflation at or below 2% every year from 1999 until 2007, albeit the margin by which the target was missed was small (much less than 1% in general) until 2008 when the eurozone inflation rate peaked at 4% in July 2008. The case for an independent Central Bank is often made on the basis of credibility in terms of achieving the inflation target. Yet the credibility of the ECB appears not to have suffered from this persistent failure.

The transmission mechanisms through which interest rates influence demand and inflationary processes differ substantially between countries. This inevitably creates difficulties in using the single instrument of the policy interest rate of the ECB to successfully target inflation rates in each of the member countries. Yet similarity of inflation rates is one of the conditions for the sustainability of a fixed exchange-rate system. When there are differences in countries' inflation rates, a perversity arises, namely that a common nominal policy rate set by the ECB translates into a lower real interest rate in a country with a higher rate of inflation, yet the theory of inflation targeting is that higher inflation should be addressed by a higher nominal and a higher real rate of interest. Thus, on this theory, differences in inflation rates are exacerbated by the common monetary policy, in effect stoking up demand in a country with higher inflation.

Although inflation targeting is focused on the interest rate/inflation dimension via demand linkages, it has become widely acknowledged (particularly since the financial crisis) that interest rates can have effects on asset prices and on exchange rates. The 'one-size-fits-all' issue feeds into aspects of the financial crisis. An example: Spain's economy grew rapidly as a construction boom developed, which in retrospect was unsustainable. This construction boom no doubt had a range of causes but low real interest rates would be supportive of such a boom. If the Spanish authorities had wished to dampen down the boom or to cope with the bust through the use of interest rates and monetary policy more generally, they were powerless to do so.

The operations of a Central Bank in many (but not all) countries involve it acting as a lender of last resort to the banking system. Further, the government does not itself directly issue money, and budget deficits have to be covered by borrowing. However, the Central Bank accepts government paper from banks as collateral for provision of reserves (at the policy rate of interest) and through that route the budget deficit could be said to be partially money financed. The Central Bank would always accept government bonds from banks – at the price which it has set. There would not be a question on the acceptability of those bonds.

When a government issues bonds in its own currency, then there is no risk of it being unable to meet its obligations on those bonds, whether in terms of interest or repayment of principal. The government possesses powers of taxation. But, more significantly, it is the Central Bank that has the ability to create money. Provided that the Central Bank creates the money (whether directly to government or indirectly through purchase of bonds), the bonds can always be repaid in the national currency. The Central Bank, if necessary under orders from its owners, the government, ensures that the bonds are repaid: in that way there is no risk of default on government bonds when they are denominated in the national currency.

The arrangements within the euro area raise problems in this regard. On the one hand, there is no fiscal policy and no budget deficit at the euro-area level. On the other hand, national governments do run budget deficits and have outstanding debts, but have to do so in a 'foreign' currency, the euro – 'foreign' in the sense that the national government and the national central bank are not able to create the currency in which the debt is denominated. It is further the case that the ECB does not have to accept the 'paper' of the national governments, and indeed had adopted a general policy of only accepting 'paper' which has achieved a high credit rating. This type of policy was suspended with the onset of the 'great recession' and when it became apparent that the role of the credit-rating agencies was rather suspect.

The ECB can, but does not have to, operate as lender of last resort. It is prohibited from monetizing government debt, but in that regard differs little from many central banks in not directly monetizing public debt, though there is the indirect monetization referred to above. The ECB has at times been slow to react to issues and problems, notably in the first weeks of the global financial crisis of autumn 2007. The issue here is not that mistakes were made but how far the ideology and policy-making framework could be held responsible. The desire to establish credibility and the focus on price stability only, and at the expense of real variables, point in the direction of a likely deflationary bias in their decision making.

Although the ECB was established as 'independent', this has not precluded it from pronouncing on macroeconomic policy and pushing a particular agenda (along the lines of fiscal consolidation and labour market 'flexibility'; see, for example, the monthly press conferences of the president of the ECB on this matter). But that very independence comes at the expense of limits on coordination of economic policy with the other institutions of the EMU and the EU. Further, the focus on price stability has meant that the effects of interest rates on exchange rate and asset prices are largely ignored.

The authorities have been left virtually powerless to address problems such as rapidly rising house prices, construction booms and the like, which contributed to the evolution of the financial crisis.

Concluding comment

The EMU and the euro area were built on a neglect of the economic requirements for the successful operation of a single currency. This did not make sufficient allowance for the institutional and economic diversities between the member states, particularly with regard to the current account imbalances and their consequences. It imposed a macroeconomic framework which had austerity tendencies with no allowance for diversity in economic conditions.

3

The Failures of the Euro Area

Introduction

Marking the first decade of the euro in 2008, the European Commission trumpeted its successful launch and operation and was generally confident of its future success, though hinting at some clouds on the horizon (European Commission 2008). In the United States, the United Kingdom and elsewhere, there was also much satisfaction in recent macroeconomic events. There was celebration of the 'great moderation' (Ben Bernanke, governor of the US Federal Reserve, and others) with lower inflation, the end of 'boom and bust' (Gordon Brown, then UK Chancellor of the Exchequer) and the NICE (non-inflationary continuous expansion) decade (Mervyn King, then governor of the Bank of England). Perspectives changed rapidly and by

2009 there was major concern over recession and euro crisis. And now a near-decade of slow growth, austerity and high unemployment has become the order of the day, along with various dimensions of the euro crisis.

The sharp changes in perceptions and performance came with the outbreak of financial crises in North America and Europe. This is often termed the 'global financial crisis', and it did indeed have international reverberations. It can also be viewed as the North Atlantic financial crisis, with the earthquake centred on the United States (but not Canada) and the United Kingdom, and major banking crises also in Ireland and Iceland. Within the euro area, most of the effects of financial crisis came from contagion: effects on many European banks were through ownership by banks of 'toxic assets', which lost value with some bank failures, and there were major effects on international trade, with dramatic falls in 2009. Some of the first evidence of a financial crisis had become evident in August 2007 with the 'freezing' of the inter-bank market and then the crisis at Northern Rock in the United Kingdom. After the near collapse and fire sale of Bears Stern in March 2008, the collapse of Lehman Brothers in September 2008 confirmed the arrival of a full-blown crisis. During September and October, major financial institutions failed, acquired under duress or subject to government takeover and bail-out in the United States, the United Kingdom, Iceland, Ireland, Belgium and the Netherlands. Spanish savings banks followed much later.

It was soon after the financial crises of 2007/9 that people started to talk of a euro crisis and the possible break-up of the euro area. One element was the perceived sovereign debt crisis in Greece. Announcements in late 2009 and early 2010 that its budget deficit figures had been understated for many years threatened to exclude the Greek government from financial markets. The so-called troika of the International Monetary Fund, the European Central Bank and the European Commission eventually issued the first of two international bail-outs for Greece, which would eventually total more than 240 billion euro. Harsh austerity measures were imposed which continue and have wrecked the Greek economy.

The financial crisis and the recession did not cause the euro crises but rather served to bring to the fore the weaknesses of the construction of the euro area and its policy agendas. The euro crises were in effect waiting to happen, and the financial crisis and recession were the trigger for the crises.

Failures of the Euro Area

In Table 3.1, a brief indication of the economic events in the euro area from 2008 through to 2015 is given. Growth was negative in 2009 and sluggish thereafter with negative growth in 2012 and 2013, and overall GDP in 2015 was 0.5% above the level of 2008. In comparison, US GDP was 10.5% higher in 2015 than in 2008, and that of the United Kingdom 7.7% higher. Unemployment rose sharply in 2009 and 2010 and has remained high (and particularly youth unemployment): again, the United States and the United Kingdom had much more favourable unemployment records. Inflation in 2011 and 2012 exceeded the 2% target, though by 2014 and 2015 deflation was much more of an issue. The current account position of the euro area moved more substantially into surplus after being close to balance during the 2000s. A notable feature of the current account position of individual countries was that those initially in deficit experienced decline in the deficits (Greece is the example in the table), whereas those in surplus continued with that position (Germany is the example here). A significant factor is that the deficit countries often experienced severe unemployment and deflation, which reduced imports, leading to the current account deficit declining. Budget deficits (relative to GDP) starting from an average of 2.2% in 2008,

Table 3.1 Economic performance in the euro area 2008–2015

	2008	2009	2010	2011	2012	2013	2014	2015
EU-19								
Growth rate (GDP annual percent)	0.3	-4.5	2.0	1.6	-0.9	-0.2	1.2	1.5
Unemployment rate (%)	7.6	9.6	10.2	10.2	11.4	12.0	11.6	10.9
Inflation (CPI: % annual rate)	3.3	0.3	1.6	2.7	2.5	1.3	0.4	0.0
Current account position (%GDP)	-0.6	0.4	0.4	0.1	2.2	2.8	3.0	3.9
(+ = surplus/– = deficit)								
Budget position (%GDP)	-2.2	-6.3	-6.2	-4.2	-3.6	-3.0	-2.6	-2.1
(+ = surplus/– = deficit)								
Germany								
Growth rate	0.8	-5.6	3.9	3.7	0.7	0.6	1.6	1.5
Unemployment	7.4	7.6	7.0	5.8	5.4	5.2	5.0	4.6
Current account position (%GDP)	5.5	5.6	5.4	6.0	7.1	6.8	7.4	8.5
(+ = surplus/– = deficit)								
Budget position (%GDP)	-0.2	-3.2	-4.2	-1.0	0.0	-0.2	0.3	0.7
(+ = surplus/– = deficit)								
Greece								
Growth rate	-0.2	-4.3	-5.5	-9.2	-7.3	-3.2	0.4	-0.3
Unemployment	7.8	9.6	12.8	17.9	24.5	27.5	26.6	25.0
Current account position (%GDP)	-15.1	-12.3	-11.4	-10.0	-3.8	-2.0	-1.6	0.1
(+ = surplus/– = deficit)								
Budget position (%GDP)	-10.2	-15.1	-11.2	-10.3	-8.8	-13.2	-3.6	-7.5
(+ = surplus/– = deficit)								

Source: OECD *Economic Outlook* 100 (November 2016)

rose to over 6% in 2009 and 2010 and have subsequently declined.

Unemployment crisis

Unemployment rose in most countries following the financial crises and the resulting recession. The euro-area construction and its policies inhibit the resolution of the unemployment crisis in at least three ways. The first is the austerity approach to fiscal policy which has been seen in the SGP and intensified by the 'fiscal compact'. The second comes from the current account imbalances within the euro area and the constraints on expansion and reduction of unemployment which they impose: and this is discussed below.

The third comes from the general approach to 'structural reforms' and the labour market. The EC had heralded the role of 'structural reforms' in reducing unemployment during the 2000s. In the celebration of the achievements of the first decade of the EMU in 2008, the claimed role of 'structural reforms' in the decline of unemployment in the first years of the euro was highlighted, as noted in chapter 1. The sharp rise in unemployment in 2009 highlighted the importance of the level of demand for employment and showed that the trumpeted 'structural reforms' had not succeeded in aiding lower unemployment. Nevertheless, following the recession, there have been pushes towards further 'structural reforms', promoted as ways to reduce unemployment. However, such 'structural reforms' do not deliver on reducing unemployment.[1]

These pressures for 'structural reform' became part of the economic policies of the EMU in 2012 with the 'fiscal compact'. Under Article 5 of the Treaty on Stability, Coordination and Governance in the Economic and Monetary Union (hereafter TSCG), 'A Contracting Party that is subject to an excessive deficit procedure under the Treaties on which the European Union is founded shall put in place a budgetary and economic partnership programme including a *detailed description of the structural reforms* which must be put in place and implemented to ensure an effective and durable correction of its excessive deficit' (European Union 2012: 14, emphasis added).

The Treaty threatens to impose neo-liberal 'structural reforms', whether or not they are appropriate to the institutional, social and political arrangements of the country concerned. It has yet to be established that a neo-liberal agenda is the appropriate one for all countries (and whether it would be acceptable to the peoples of the countries). Indeed, 'all countries affected by the crisis and subjected to structural adjustment have moved a step closer to the liberal model . . .' (Hermann 2014: 125).

The EC has often promoted supply-side policies, and notably 'structural reforms', as a way of promoting employment. The then European Commission president, José Manuel Barroso, argued that the EU member states 'should now intensify their efforts on structural reforms for competitiveness'. He specifically highlighted the need for comprehensive labour market reforms as 'the best way to kick-start job creation' (Press Conference, Brussels, 29 May 2013). In a similar vein, the ECB frequently calls for fiscal consolidation and 'structural reforms' to stimulate economic performance.[2]

Hermann (2014) shows how European countries responded to the financial crisis in terms of reductions in social spending and through labour market reforms with cuts to minimum wages, flexibilization of working time, reductions in employment protection and changes in collective bargaining. The EC, the ECB and the IMF played pivotal roles in the adoption of austerity and structural reforms across the European Union. When countries were receiving emergency loans from the European Stability Mechanism and/or from the IMF, the envisaged reforms were included in the Memoranda of Understanding negotiated between the troika of the EC, the ECB and the IMF and the national governments as a condition of receiving the emergency funds.

The promotion of a 'structural reform' agenda as the route to higher levels of employment in the EMU (and more widely) is flawed in at least three ways. The first is that the promotion of what is a common agenda of neo-liberal reforms does not take any cognizance of the differences in labour market institutions, practices and policies between countries. It runs the danger of falling foul of the problems of a 'one size fits all' approach.

The second is that the 'structural reforms' agenda promotes the deregulation of labour (and other markets), even though the evidence does not support the view that such markets work better than regulated ones.[3]

The third is that it also incorporates a view that 'structural reforms' somehow bring economic recovery. However, many of the measures associated with labour flexibility (such as a more stringent approach to unemployment benefits and the reduction of minimum wages) would tend to reduce the wage share in national income, to depress demand and to increase the budget deficit (Tridico 2012).

The budget deficit could then only be expected to decline (following a more 'flexible' labour market) if an investment boom were stimulated.

Will 'structural reforms' bring economic prosperity? Will they bring jobs? It is treated as obvious, by neo-liberals, that deregulated labour markets – reduced job protections, more 'flexible' (lower) wages – will bring more jobs. If that were so, however, then reducing wages to close to zero should bring a boom! The difficulty with that is immediately apparent: if wages are very low, who buys what is produced? Further, is it really the case that for workers to be engaged with their work and well motivated, the lower the pay, the better? Policies designed to reduce wages will likely increase unemployment – particularly when such reductions are taking place in a range of countries. Evidence supports the view that economies are wage-led rather than profit-led, and hence that lowering wages would reduce demand and raise unemployment (see, for example, Lavoie and Stockhammer 2013). Lower wages in a country may boost exports but, in a relatively closed economy such as the European Union, that effect is likely to be small. We can share the view of Capaldo and Izurieta (2013): '[P]ursuing labour market flexibilization with the aim of increasing employment via export-driven growth is bound to fail, especially if fiscal austerity prevents government spending from picking up the slack in global demand' (p. 23).

Fiscal policy responses

In the immediate aftermath of the financial crisis in late 2008, the budget deficits of the national governments of the euro area rose as the recession bit. This could be seen as the usual occurrence during recession as tax revenues decline, and allowed the 'automatic stabilizers' to operate to some degree. The SGP permitted increases in the budget deficit, though in many cases the deficit broke through the 3 per cent upper limit of the SGP. This reflected the severity of the recession and that many countries were starting from a position of significant budget deficit (despite the SGP). Instead of adopting the position of encouraging an economic recovery and a subsequent decline in the budget deficits, the response was to blame the pre-crisis levels of deficit and debt for the crisis and to tighten the constraints on budget deficits and increase the pressures to seek a balanced budget, whatever the costs of so doing. The push towards fiscal consolidation and austerity can be seen in terms of the structural budget position (which in principle is not affected by the trade-cycle position): for the euro area as a whole, this declined from a deficit of 4.26 per cent of GDP in 2010 to 1.04 per cent in 2015.[4] In policy terms, the result was the 'fiscal compact'. This was essentially agreed in December 2011, reflecting perceptions that there had been a general failure to observe the SGP, which had led to significant budget deficits in many countries even prior to the financial crisis. Immediately after the financial crisis, budget deficits and debt ratios rose rapidly as the automatic stabilizers of fiscal policy took effect. The scale of the budget deficits during recession was interpreted in terms of a failure to maintain the rules of the SGP for a budget balanced over the cycle, and for allowing debt ratios at or above the 60 per cent threshold, and the perception left limited room for man-oeuvre during recession. The 'fiscal compact' can be viewed as an ordo-liberal response to the financial crisis and recession (as discussed in chapter 5) in that the deficit requirement has now to be written into each country's national constitution or equivalent. It can be argued that this is democratic in that the parliament of the country concerned has rati-fied the TSCG, but it does mean that any member government which wishes to depart from pursuit of structural balanced budget faces legal constraints and inhibits political parties campaigning for a break with austerity.

The key attributes of the approach to fiscal policy within the euro area following the adoption of the 'fiscal compact' are twofold, and those attributes are at the heart of the austerity regime.

1 It is organized around the idea of a balanced structural budget. These proposals are critiqued below, and the ways in which this approach favours austerity are highlighted.
2 The 'excessive deficit procedure' (EDP) is an action launched by the European Commission against any EU member state (and hence including those countries which are not members of the euro area) deemed to have excessive deficit. The procedure can culminate in sanctions against the member country.

Under the 'fiscal compact', a stricter policy was imposed on countries with a debt ratio exceeding 60% of GDP. The Treaty makes it possible to open an 'excessive deficit procedure'. To avoid being placed in the 'excessive deficit procedure', member states with government debt ratios in excess of 60% of their GDP should reduce this ratio in line with a numerical benchmark, which implies a decline in the amount by which their debt exceeds the threshold at a rate in the order of one-twentieth per year over three years. However, in a slow growth economy with a debt ratio of, say, 120% of GDP, this approach would involve a budget surplus of the order of 3% of GDP (and a primary surplus which is substantially greater when interest payments on debt are considered). While the choice of the 60% figure has appeared before – in the convergence criteria in the SGP – it is quite arbitrary and reflects little more than the German debt ratio in the early 1990s.

The 'fiscal compact' imposes the pursuit of a 'balanced structural budget'.[5] A structural budget position is that which would arise with the present pattern of tax rates and government expenditure *if* the economy were operating at 'potential output'. In turn, 'potential output' is the level of output at which inflation would tend to be constant and can be thought to correspond to the 'non-accelerating rate of inflation'.

It can first be noted that to arrive at the 'structural budget position' requires a number of hypothetical calculations which place the evaluation of budget plans in the hands of the technocrats undertaking the calculations. The second point, which reinforces the first, is that 'potential output' (and the corresponding non-accelerating inflation rate of unemployment: NAIRU) is a theoretical construct which may or may not be a good representation of the real world. It requires, for example, that there exist a level of potential output that is consistent with constant inflation, and that does not depend on other economic variables. The estimation of 'potential output' depends on past data and on which econometric techniques are used and, as indicated in an ECB publication (Jarocinski and Lenza 2016), for example, many alternative estimates are possible.

A further and significant element is the tendency for the estimates of 'potential output' to follow actual output. This can be emphasized by the estimates of the non-accelerating inflation rate of unemployment. Figure 3.1 tracks one set of estimates for Spain. It can be seen that the NAIRU follows actual unemployment, and that a period of high unemployment raises the estimate of the NAIRU. Consider the estimate of the NAIRU for Spain for 2015: the OECD *Economic Outlook* in December 2016 gives a figure for 2015 of 15.9%, though the estimate given in OECD *Economic Outlook* June 2015 was 18.6%. The structural budget position is calculated from such an estima-

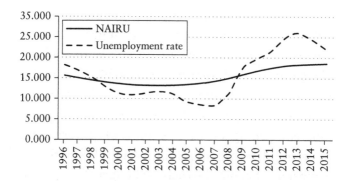

Figure 3.1 Unemployment and the NAIRU in Spain, 1996–2015 (%)

Source: OECD *Economic Outlook*, various issues

tion. Now consider if that estimate is incorrect, or if the estimate of the NAIRU would change with the experience of lower unemployment or if the NAIRU is not accepted as an appropriate benchmark (and, rather, a benchmark of full employment was used), then the structural budget estimate would be way off. It could well be the case that using an unemployment rate benchmark of 5%, rather than one of 16%, would transform an estimate of structural budget position by the order of 5–6% of GDP. Rather than requiring drastic cuts to public expenditure in search of a budget balance, it would require large increases in public expenditure or tax reductions to bring the surplus down.

To postulate that a country has to achieve a balanced structural budget (and, indeed, that all member countries have to do so) is to make a giant leap of faith that it is achievable. It can also be observed that countries have a tendency to run structural budget deficits. This could be a sign of inherent profligacy on the part of government, or it could be an indication of the difficulties of achieving a balanced structural budget. The general difficulty of achieving a balanced budget can be seen by reference to equation (1) in the previous chapter.

Debt issues

Although euro-area member countries were in principle constrained to have public debt less than the equivalent of 60% of GDP, the average debt ratio for the euro-area countries was 65% in 2007 and 68.8% in 2008, with the debt ratios in 2007 varying from below 4% in Estonia (at that time not yet a member of the euro area), below 8% in Luxembourg through to 99.8% (Italy) and 103.1% (Greece), with seven countries exceeding the 60% debt ratio limit. The debt ratios rose substantially following the 'great recession'.

The newly elected government in Greece revealed a budget deficit and government debt levels much higher than had previously been thought. For example, the debt-to-GDP ratio for 2008 had been thought to be 101.1%, but was raised to 116%; corresponding figures for budget deficit were 5% and 9.8%.[6] Budget deficits were in any case rising under the impact of the recession. These budget deficit figures reinforced the degree to which deficits had not met the requirements of the SGP. In some cases, budget deficits and outstanding debt were swollen by the bail-out of banks (Ireland being the most notable example, with a budget deficit running at more than 32% of GDP in 2010 as compared with a small budget surplus in 2007).

The treatment applied to Greece has been disastrous for the people of Greece[7] – the unemployment and decline of income are indicated in Table 3.1. Greece has felt the full brunt of the austerity obsession of the SGP and now the 'fiscal compact'. The ECB's reluctance to purchase Greek government bonds and the constraints on any direct financing of budget deficits intensified the problems. Within a single currency, government (and indeed private) debt is denominated in euros, which in a number of respects is a 'foreign' currency as far as the national government is concerned. The ECB is not only prohibited from the direct financing of budget deficits but is also under no obligation to purchase a government's outstanding debt.

The imposition of austerity, requirements for budget cuts, the forms which they took and the 'structural reforms' were accompanied by claims that they would be the route to restoring employment and prosperity.[8] Those policies have been spectacular failures – as the figures in Table 3.1 suggest. The budget deficit has indeed been cut but no recovery has come about.

Current account issues

The current account imbalances among euro-area members had tended to widen in the decade prior to 2008 (as indicated in chapter 2), and a continuing widening of those imbalances would not have been sustainable. The financial crisis brought these issues on the current account imbalances to the fore. A current account deficit has to be covered by borrowing from abroad, and the financial crisis made such borrowing much more difficult.

The original Treaty of Rome included an article which required member states to pursue economic policies to ensure the equilibrium of their overall balance of payments, to maintain confidence in their currency, and to seek a high level of employment and a stable level of prices. The Treaty of Maastricht repealed this article, and now current account imbalances are central to the problems of the euro area (Smith 2016). It is rather shocking that there was no attention given to the current account position of a country in the convergence criteria of the Treaty of Maastricht, nor to the current account imbalances between the founding member countries of the EMU.

The ECB (2007) was able to stress the challenges and risks presented by the magnitude of global imbalances and the need for appropriate policy actions. Yet it could do so without any reference to the imbalances within the euro area which were amongst the largest deficits (as percentage of GDP) in the world (for example, Spain) and the largest surpluses (for example, Germany). And the current account imbalances between the euro-area member states are particularly difficult to resolve as exchange rate adjustment between the member states is clearly not possible.

In 2010, a paper in *European Economy*, the journal of the Directorate of Economic and Financial Affairs, recognized that divergences in competitiveness between countries of the euro and imbalances impacted adversely on the functioning of the EMU. It was then argued that 'Large losses in competitiveness combined with persistent accumulation of large current deficits cannot be sustained forever and can be reversed only at the cost of protracted periods of painful adjustment' (European Commission 2010: 13). There had been divergence in competitiveness during the 2000s adding to the current account imbalances. The corresponding capital flows were often contributing to rapid growth of household borrowing, credit and housing price booms. 'In current account deficit countries, large capital inflows led to an unsustainable accumulation of household and corporate debt, in some countries aggravated by an inappropriate response of fiscal policy. In some Member States, the accumulation of large current account surpluses reflected structural weaknesses in domestic demand' (European Commission 2010: 13).

Inflation had been lower than hitherto, but differences between countries remained. This had implications for trade competitiveness. Whether as a direct result of those differential trends in competitiveness or not, there were clear divergences in the current account deficits – also in differences in growth rates of imports and exports. Movement of the value of the euro, and particularly its rise in value against the dollar after 2002, may have differential effects as exports of some countries are less sensitive to price changes than those of other countries.

A country's ability to run a current account deficit depends on its ability to borrow from external sources, that is, to run a capital-account surplus. A country in a fixed exchange-rate regime can run an overall balance-of-payments deficit, provided that it possesses sufficient foreign exchange reserves to meet that deficit – but of course the foreign exchange reserves could soon be exhausted with a persistent balance-of-payments deficit. In the context of the euro currency union, a country can run a balance-of-payments deficit for some while. A balance-of-payments deficit in one country implies that the reserves of that country's central bank held at the ECB are falling, and correspondingly the reserves of other countries' central banks are rising. There are, again, limits on how long that could continue.

The focus then is on the scale of current account deficit which can be funded through overseas borrowing. The key question which faces a number of euro-area countries (Greece and Portugal, for example) is: if the economy were to operate at high levels of output and employment, what would the resulting current account position be, and would the people of that country be able to collectively borrow from external sources? In other words, is there a balance-of-payments constraint which effectively precludes anything resembling full employment, even if there were sufficient demand and sufficient productive capacity to support full employment?

The current account positions of the euro-area member countries continue to be problematic and serve to place major constraints on many of them returning to prosperity. The notion of balance of payments constraining growth indicates that those with low income elasticity for their exports and/ or high income elasticity for imports are likely to be constrained to relatively low growth. For many countries, moves towards full employment and higher incomes would involve substantial current account deficits which would have to be financed through capital inflows.

Estimates of the degree of misalignment of the real exchange rates between the member countries of the euro in light of the differences in their prices have been made, e.g. by Mazier and Petit (2013). Coudert, Couharde and Mignon (2013) provide estimates of currency misalignments with the euro area using a 'behavioural equilibrium exchange rate' as the benchmark. They find misalignments of currencies since the formation of the monetary union for eight out of the eleven euro members reviewed. On average, the misalignments are larger in each period for peripheral countries, as well as Finland. The increase in misalignments has been particularly marked in Greece, Ireland and Portugal. The authors also indicate (pp. 44–5) that the misalignments are more persistent after monetary union than before, and that they are more persistent in the peripheral countries than in the core members.

The devaluation option is limited in the context of a single currency as it would require lower domestic prices, though it could be aided by inflation in the surplus countries. The effectiveness of any 'internal devaluation' is limited in so far as price elasticities are relatively low and/or there is limited productive capacity to meet any increase in export demand.

In the context of the euro area, however, a member country's ability to devalue in real terms is limited and fiscal transfers are virtually non-existent. The balance-of-payments position in a number of countries threatens to consign some countries to prolonged periods of unemployment and slow growth. Those countries can only escape those constraints with large-scale investment and industrial development. Investment undertaken wisely can provide the capacity to produce exports and thereby ease the balance-of-payments issues. In a similar vein, industrial policies are required to mould the industrial structure in ways which are conducive to growth and enable the balance-of-payments-constrained growth rate to be raised. The problems of formulating and implementing such policies are substantial and always require funding. Yet, if such policies are not implemented, the prospects for many euro-area countries are indeed bleak.

The role of the ECB and its response to financial crises

The difficulties with the position of the ECB can be grouped under two headings. The first is the intensification of the 'one size fits all' problem facing any central bank, and the second is the nature of its relationship with national governments and the absence of a federal fiscal authority.

The 'one size fits all' problem at its most general demonstrates complications which arise from application of a single policy measure across diverse situations. In the case of monetary policy, this is the requirement for a single policy interest rate to be set which applies across all of the regions of the monetary area. Yet the circumstances of one region may suggest a relatively high interest rate (say, to dampen down demand) and of another region a relatively low interest rate. In the context of the euro, this problem is exacerbated (as compared with a relatively small country) by the scale of the area and the extent of the diversity of member economies, including institutional arrangements.

The ECB is charged with achieving price stability, which it has interpreted as inflation (across the euro area) below 2 per cent per annum. The policy instrument is the interest rate(s) set by the ECB. In principle, the ECB should support more general policies on employment and output, but its focus has been on inflation. There have been two difficulties here. First, as argued extensively elsewhere (Arestis and Sawyer 2008), interest-rate policy is an ineffective instrument for the control of inflation.

Second, it could do nothing to address differences in inflation between the member countries. The ECB is set up as an 'independent' central bank, independent, that is, in terms of political and democratic control, though not in an ideological sense. This is seen in their constant calls for fiscal consolidation and for so-called 'structural reforms'. This so-called independence does make coordination of macroeconomic policies problematic. The responses of the ECB to the financial crisis and the recession have often been seen as 'too little, too late', particularly in comparison with the US Federal Reserve and the Bank of England.[9] Changes occurred in July 2012 when Mario Draghi, president of the ECB, declared he would do 'whatever it takes' (Draghi 2012) to save the euro. The ECB then stated that it would purchase unlimited amounts of national debt on secondary markets but with the proviso that the countries in question agree to reform programmes negotiated with the troika. This is not the place to undertake a detailed critique of the policies of the ECB: it is rather to see how the structure and policy outlook of the ECB contributed to the euro crisis. A significant component was that the ECB was reluctant to act as a lender of last resort for sovereign governments.

Existential crisis

In his 'State of the Union' speech in September 2016, following the UK referendum result for the United Kingdom to leave the EU, Jean-Claude Juncker declared that 'Our European Union is, at least in part, in an existential crisis.' Many others have spoken since around 2010 of an existential crisis surrounding the future of the euro. It is evident that many of the euro-area countries face severe unemployment problems, which are exacerbated by their membership of the euro area. The austerity macroeconomic policies of the euro area and the current account imbalances and misaligned real exchange rates have intensified the problems of the euro area.

Many fixed exchange-rate systems have dissolved when the tensions within them became unsustainable. There are always limits on a country running a balance-of-payments deficit which is only funded by a depletion of its foreign exchange reserves. When the foreign reserves run out, eventually something has to give. And that something is exit of the country concerned from the fixed exchange-rate system. Many of the countries of the euro area are now in a situation where a return to anything like full employment is ruled out as it would not be possible to borrow to cover the current account deficit which would arise at a high level of employment. In addition, membership of the euro area imposes pursuit of balanced structural budgets which are unfeasible – a balanced budget may be achievable through sufficient austerity (though even that is doubtful) but a budget balanced at full employment is not.

71

4

An Agenda for Prosperity

Introduction[1]

The economic difficulties besetting the euro area have a range of causes. Some can be ascribed to the behaviours and actions of the major participants, including the European Commission, the European Central Bank, national governments and others, particularly in response to the financial crisis. The focus, however, should be on what may be termed the 'design faults' of the EMU (Arestis and Sawyer 2011) with its ordo-liberal agenda of 'independent' central banking and detachment of the European Central Bank (ECB) from national governments, the prime objective being inflation and not employment or output. The nature of the convergence criteria and the SGP, reinforced by the 'fiscal compact', imposes a generally deflationary atmosphere, even if the budget deficit constraints are often not adhered to. The formation of the euro paid attention to convergence of inflation, but not to wage- and price-setting institutions. The construction of the EMU paid virtually no attention to current account imbalances, the relationships between deficit countries and surplus countries, or the ways in which those imbalances would be resolved. It is notable that while limits on budget deficits appear among the convergence criteria of the Maastricht Treaty, current account deficits do not. No regard was paid to whether the initial current account imbalances would be sustainable or how adjustments to resolve the imbalances would be undertaken. The current account imbalances implied corresponding capital-account flows. In the first decade of the eurozone, current account imbalances tended to widen, with deficit countries able to finance their deficit through capital inflows and associated credit booms.

The euro area faces two essential and interconnected policy problems. The first is that the policy framework governing the euro area (notably the SGP and the 'fiscal compact') is a 'bad' one. The second is how to adopt policies which are tailored to the needs of constructing a single currency.

The conditions for an operational currency union may well include a system of fiscal transfers, direct or indirect, between the constituent components of the currency union. Further, similarities of policy outlooks and institutional arrangements which favour the operation of a currency union are more likely to happen within a long-standing political union (though there is no inevitability of, for example, similarity of policy outlook across component parts of a political union). The workings of the euro area would be enhanced by a range of measures, such as fiscal transfers between nations, development of unemployment insurance arrangements in a coordinated direction, addressing current account imbalances through regional and industrial policies and so on, which would in effect represent steps in the direction of political integration between the member states and 'ever closer union'.

Fiscal rules

In a nation-state, the single currency of that state is accompanied by many policy arrangements, including fiscal and monetary policy. A single currency necessarily has a corresponding central bank operating a single monetary policy – in terms of policy interest rate (and if there were a target for the growth of the money supply, that would also apply across the currency area). In a nation-state, the central bank is the bank of the central government and the bank of the banks. In the first of those roles, there is a close relationship between the central bank and the operation of fiscal policy. The government holds its account at the central bank and draws on that account in order to finance its expenditure. That account is replenished through the receipt of tax revenues and from the proceeds of sales of government bonds. The central bank is supportive of government policy in always being prepared to purchase (from the market) government bonds.

Fiscal policy can play a significant role in the stabilization and achievement of high levels of economic activity. There should be two basic principles underlying the approach to fiscal policy within the EMU. Firstly, the fiscal stance should be set to enhance the levels of output and employment, and not set in order to achieve some arbitrary budget target when that target may not be achievable. There must not be any attempt to impose a 'one size fits all' fiscal policy on national government in the sense of imposing the same numerical limits on the scale of budget deficits (whether a zero limit or any other). The fiscal policy and resulting budget position should be tailored to the requirements of the country concerned: some countries will require budget deficits whereas others may be able to operate successfully with budget surpluses. The current account positions vary substantially across countries, and allowance must be made for that. A policy shift which interpreted the budget constraints in terms of the current budget and thus permitted borrowing for public investment would ease the present constraints. At present, deficit limits apply to the total budget and hence serve to constrain public investment, even in countries which have strong requirements for such investments.

Second, there needs to be a recognition of the role of federal fiscal policies in monetary unions such as the United States. This would require a substantial EMU (or EU) budget much larger than the current EU budget (of just over 1 per cent of EU GDP, and with a requirement to be balanced). A federal fiscal policy has some potential for stabilizing economic activity, specifically in terms of helping to cushion downturns in individual regions and countries.

It is well known that a progressive tax system acts as an automatic stabilizer (that is, tax revenues rise, relative to level of income, when national income rises and fall when national income falls). A progressive tax system also operates to transfer resources from high-income areas (where tax payments to the central authority are relatively high) to low-income areas. It is, of course, such transfers between countries, where high-income countries pay more, that would lead to one of the major political obstacles to a federal fiscal policy.

There are roles for schemes along the lines of a 'EU Infrastructure Investment Plan' (often referred to as the Juncker Plan, announced by European Commission President Jean-Claude Juncker in November 2014) which is aimed at raising public and private investment.[2] These schemes can bypass the attempted constraints on fiscal deficits, as they are operated in effect 'off balance sheet', so far as the member countries are concerned. For example, the European Investment Bank borrows from the capital markets and then lends on to public and private institutions to fund the latter's investment programmes.

A federal fiscal policy would be a significant step in the direction of political union as it would have important features such as tax-raising powers, undertaking public expenditure and the ability to run budget deficits (or surpluses) at the federal level. These are, of course, activities of a political nature being undertaken at the federal union and representing an element of political union. It would require the support of the ECB in the operation of fiscal policy and a willingness to buy where the bonds are issued by that federal authority.

Federal taxation

The development of federal fiscal policy obviously requires the development of federal tax revenues – whether collected by national authorities on behalf of the EU or by the EU itself. It would be feasible to develop tax revenues on a similar basis to that which operates with respect to Value-Added Tax (VAT), whereby there are agreed limits such that the minimum VAT general rate is 15 per cent, though there are variations on taxable items (e.g. food may be zero-rated, subject to a lower rate).

The development of federal taxation should be done in ways which aid the functioning of the single market and include a federal approach to corporate profits tax (to ease tax competition and reduce evasion through transfer pricing) and the construction of an EU-wide social security system, starting with unemployment benefits.

An Agenda for Prosperity

The European Central Bank

The present status of the European Central Bank (ECB) was set out in the section on the European Central Bank in chapter 2 as an 'independent' (of political influence) central bank with price stability as its key objective. This status of the ECB is enshrined (now) in the Treaty of Lisbon, and as such is only changeable unanimously by the national governments (and others). The changes to the operations of the ECB fall under four broad headings.

First, significant changes would be required in the objectives of the European Central Bank. The policy objectives should be broadened beyond the price stability objective in two directions: to acknowledge the aim of high and sustainable levels of employment; and to incorporate financial stability. The experience of the 1990s and 2000s, when inflation targeting was the 'conventional wisdom' for central banks, has been that the use of the policy interest rate to achieve low inflation is not particularly effective. And in the single currency area, monetary policy was not able (and indeed could not be expected) to address differences in inflationary experience between countries (as discussed in chapter 2).

A major lesson which should be learnt from the experiences of the 2000s is that the price stability that would be necessary and sufficient for financial and macroeconomic stability does not hold. Interest rates, which were intended to be set to pursue price stability, affect asset prices and financial stability. There is little reason to think that these side effects of interest rates used for inflation targeting will be benign. It has to be recognized that the policy instruments at the disposal of the ECB, namely the policy interest rate (supplemented by quantitative easing), are not particularly effective and specifically suffer from 'one size fits all' problems.

Second, the so-called political independence of the ECB should be ended and it should be required to coordinate with other policy agencies. Operational decisions would remain with the central bank (in ways which were in wide use prior to the mania for independent central banks).

Third, the ECB must act to support rather than undermine the fiscal policies of member countries (and in due course that of the federal EMU budget). In effect, the ECB must come to act in relation to national governments in the manner in which a national central bank generally does in respect of support of its government's fiscal policy through the required supply of central bank money and purchase of government bonds.

Fourth, the ECB should on all occasions stand ready to operate as 'lender of last resort'. It should always accept the bonds and bills issued by national governments (within the EMU) as part of open-market operations in the way in which a national central bank would always accept the bonds of its government. It should also stand ready to directly lend to national governments (in exchange for bonds in euros of that government) if required. The general proposition is that the ECB should support the fiscal policies determined by EMU national governments, whether or not those policies involve deficits of which the ECB disapproves.

Financial policies

Commercial banks are the major creators of money and provide the means by which money moves from one individual to another. A basic requirement for a currency union is coordinated regulation and over-sight of the banking systems. The financial crisis highlighted issues over banking and its regulation in the framework of a single market and currency and of the free movement of capital. It also reinforced the notion that a currency union (along with capital mobility) should be accompanied by common approaches to banking and its regulation.

The creation of a European banking union, developed from 2012, represents a significant move towards integration. The largest banks are supervised directly by the ECB, and the national supervisors monitor other banks. There is also the Single Resolution Mechanism (SRM) which applies to banks covered by the Single Supervisory Mechanism (SSM). This mechanism is financed by the banking sector and allows bank resolution to be managed through a Single Resolution Board. The European Deposit Insurance Scheme (EDIS) would apply to deposits below 100,000 euros of all banks in the euro area. When a bank is placed into insolvency or in resolution and it is necessary to pay out deposits or to finance their transfer to another bank, the national deposit guarantee schemes and the EDIS will intervene. The purpose of the EDIS is to ensure equal protection of deposits through the Banking Union, regardless of the member state where the deposit is located. The development of the European Banking Union is illustrative of a move towards integration in support of the single currency, with regulation of the larger banks shifting from the national to the federal level (in the form of the ECB). It also illustrates that issues of subsidiarity have to be tackled – that is, which elements of policy implementation are allocated to the federal level and which to the national level. Issues also arise on the formulation of federal-level banking regulation, which has to bring some uniformity across the diversity of the national banking regulations, and how that formulation respects the differences of banking structures between countries.

Current account imbalances

One requirement for the sustainability of a fixed exchange-rate system (and a currency union is a fixed exchange-rate system par excellence) is that rates of inflation are broadly similar across the member states. The disparities of inflation and inflationary conditions were outlined above. There is no current policy to address inflation differentials, and the current monetary policy, which is intended to target the average rate of inflation across the euro area, cannot do so. Indeed, if anything, inflation targeting makes matters worse – a country with relatively high inflation would have low, if not negative, real rates of interest, and very low real interest rates would tend to raise demand, cause inflation and promote credit booms. There is a need for a coordinated approach and common inflation targets to be addressed by national policies. This would not be 'inflation targeting', if that term is understood to mean an inflation objective pursued by an independent central bank through interest rates. It would rather be a coordinated attempt by the member states of the EMU to use their own national policies to achieve a common rate of inflation to avoid inflation differences. This could take the form of using fiscal policy to vary demand – not to be recommended, but possible. It could take the form of national agreements on incomes and prices. What has to be avoided is competitive devaluation of real exchange rates (between EMU member countries) achieved through hyper-low inflation. There should be a requirement to coordinate prices and wages policies between countries to seek to address the differential developments in competitiveness which have been evident.

For a country to have high levels of employment requires, inter alia, that there is sufficient productive capacity to support a high level of employment and that the current account position which arises with a high level of employment is sustainable. A current account deficit (resulting from imports exceeding exports) can be maintained provided that borrowing from overseas (on the capital account) can be readily undertaken. Even then, there is the issue that the interest payments and similar on the borrowing have to be made in the future, adding to the current account deficit. There are then limits to how far a country can go in running current account deficits over a prolonged period. The current account imbalances within the euro area of the late 2000s have diminished; specifically, current account deficits have diminished. But the reductions in current account deficits have come at great cost, with deflation and austerity used to drive down imports.

The return to prosperity within the euro area in a way which includes all countries and regions requires that the current account imbalances be resolved. The move towards a sustainable pattern of current account positions would involve some form of effective devaluation and revaluation within the euro area, even if there is scepticism over the effectiveness of devaluation in addressing a current account deficit, not to mention the costs and difficulties in securing such devaluation through internal deflation. Since, in the context of the EMU having an overall current account position close to balance, one country's surplus is another country's deficit, a further requirement would be a degree of agreement on the pattern of current account positions.

The major requirement, however, is that there is the creation of capacity and competitiveness in countries and regions that are less prosperous and are facing current account deficit issues. The policy developments which are required are those which come under the heading of regional and structural policies and industrial policies. There is already a strong case for the development and enhancement of industrial and regional policies within the EU designed to address the disparities in economic performance between the member states, which, if successfully implemented, would enhance the workings of the single currency. The particular importance of regional and industrial policies in the setting of a single currency arises from addressing the differences in competitiveness between countries, enabling a resolution of the current account imbalances through capacity construction in deficit countries.

Regional policies are already in operation within the EU, albeit on a rather small scale. The Structural Funds, amounting to 0.4 per cent of EU GDP, provide programmes intended to address imbalances at the regional level. The European Fund for Strategic Investments (EFSI), established in 2015, is an initiative launched jointly by the EIB Group and the European Commission to mobilize private financing for strategic investments. It is important to build on such initiatives. They can provide ways of funding public investment outside of the constraints of the SGP and facilitate investment in those countries and regions which encounter difficulties in borrowing from international capital markets.

The approach in industrial policy within the EU has involved a competition and mergers policy (from the Treaty of Rome) that has become increasingly EU-wide in application, the promotion of liberalization, particularly with regard to public utilities, and limits on state aid. There has been rather limited development of EU-wide industrial policies through the promotion of research and development, but notoriously there has been little if any progress in the aim to 'make Europe, by 2010, the most competitive and the most dynamic knowledge-based economy in the world', as set out in the Lisbon Strategy of 2000. There has been something of a revival of interest in industrial policies and strategies, though at present without any significant policy shift. For example, at the time of writing, the UK government has launched a consultation exercise on industrial strategy, though it remains to be seen whether that consultation leads to a serious industrial strategy – a term which has many meanings. The approach to industrial policy which would be advocated here would follow Pianta (2016) when he states, 'the rationale for industrial policy is that it can steer the evolution of the economy towards activities that are desirable in economic terms (improving efficiency), in social terms (addressing needs and reducing inequality), in environmental terms (assuring sustainability) and in political terms (protecting key national interests)' (2016: 139). He then advocates a public investment and infrastructure programme which targets new fields whose development is desirable in economic and social terms as well as environmental terms. Authors such as Aiginger (2016), Pianta, Lucchese and Nascia (2016) and the symposium Mazzucato et al. (2015) develop ideas for European industrial policies. The significant elements of such approaches to industrial policy are the nature and scale of government intervention, the focus on investment in infrastructure and in research and development, and the possible roles of industrial policy in addressing issues of environmental sustainability and inequalities, particularly between regions. 'Industrial policy formulation and execution have to take place at all levels (regional and sub-regional, national and supra-national' (Landesmann 2015: 138), and

Landesmann indicates the factors to be taken into account when thinking of the appropriate level and the degree of coordination involved. These all raise tricky issues of subsidiarity and coordination in the EU setting.

There are a number of funding programmes in the Europe 2020 strategy, which the EC describes as 'the current EU agenda for growth and jobs' (https://ec.europa.eu/info/strategy/european-semester/framework/europe-2020-strategy-en) relevant to European industrial policy (Pianta, Lucchese and Nascia 2016: Table 2).[3] However, the emphasis on fiscal consolidation and austerity within euro-area countries has 'further sidelined any serious discussion on industrial policy. The goals of Europe 2020 are now reinterpreted in line with the neo-liberal view that economic growth can be supported by the operation of markets and that fiscal consolidation and debt reduction create appropriate conditions for long-term growth' (Pianta, Lucchese and Nascia 2016: 42). The reorientation of industrial policy which is sought is one supported by investment and fiscal expansion, with governments at different levels involved in strategy formulation and addressing issues of environmental sustainability and regional disparities.

An Agenda for Prosperity

Labour market and welfare policies

There are, of course, no legal constraints on the movement of people within and between countries in the broader European Union, although migration has generated political resistance, often taking the form of the rise of right-wing anti-immigrant political movements and parties. While there has been the removal of formal barriers to labour movement, and encouragement through, for example, interchangeability of qualifications, there have not been serious attempts to create what could be viewed as a European labour market. What has not been addressed within the EU (and hence within the EMU) to any real extent is the development of an EU-wide social security system and income support, or some degree of compatibility between national social security systems.

A step in the direction of a federal social security system and one which would also aid stabilization would be the adoption of a European-level unemployment insurance scheme.[4] A European unemployment insurance scheme would provide a fiscal stimulus to an economy undergoing a cyclical downturn. It could help to support domestic demand and economic growth (see, for example, former European Commissioner for

Employment and Social Affairs, László Andor (Andor 2014)).

A significant feature of the Treaty on Stability, Coordination and Governance in the Economic and Monetary Union is the role given to 'structural reforms' (for which read deregulation, liberalization and privatization) and the associated view that there is 'best practice' and the suitability of a single set of policy measures on labour and product markets. The starting point for an alternative policy framework would be the removal of the general presumption of the superiority of neo-liberal policies.

The single currency obviously imposes the ultimate in a fixed exchange-rate regime, and the supply-side policies have to take cognizance of that. In the area of labour market policies, this would suggest (as above) a degree of coordination across countries with regard to wage and price increases. The major differences between nations in institutional arrangements and historical experience suggest that attempts to impose a common set of policies is inappropriate and liable to fail, but that it cannot be left to 'market forces' to iron out inflation and competitiveness differentials.

The policies towards the labour market and industrial policy require major shifts. There should be a commitment to the encouragement of progressive labour market policies and dropping of the promotion of so-called 'structural reforms'.

Would a 'northern euro'/'southern euro' be a way out?

The type of policies outlined above would clearly involve a direction of travel towards 'more Europe' and strong elements of moves towards de facto political union. In the next chapter, the formidable obstacles to the developments, such as those advanced here, are considered. For those who view the problems and difficulties of the euro area as stemming from a combination of inappropriate real exchange rates between the member countries and diversity of institutional and policy perspectives, one approach which has been advanced is for moves to a 'northern euro' and a 'southern euro'.

Stiglitz (2016), for example, envisages a 'northern euro' and a 'southern euro', with the 'southern euro' being a continuation of the euro itself and the 'northern euro' anticipated to appreciate against the euro, helping to diminish the current account surpluses of northern European countries. This arrangement would help to reduce the problems arising from the denomination of debts in euros in a country adopting a currency whose value depreciates against the euro. The diversity of current account positions in northern Europe (notably France with its current account deficit) would mean that a uniform depreciation would still leave current account imbalances.

However, a 'northern euro'/'southern euro' system would still face many problems, and indeed would do little to resolve the acute problems facing the euro area. Four particular sets of issues are highlighted here.

The first is the issue of national memberships of the 'northern euro' and of the 'southern euro'. The optimal currency area (OCA) literature and the more general considerations of the economic, institutional and policy similarities and divergences between potential members could form the basis for addressing that issue. The Maastricht Treaty identified convergence criteria for membership of the euro, but these were inadequate in that they addressed conditions at a point in time (e.g. convergence of the rate of inflation rather than of the inflationary processes), and failed to address important dimensions of convergence (e.g. sustainability of current account positions and of the business cycle). Further, there appears to have been little thought given to the compatibilities of institutional arrangements. The lessons of the failures of the euro could be valuable here. However, the nature of those lessons would no doubt be a matter of great dispute. Drawing up any criteria for membership runs into the obvious difficulty that a country seeking to be a member of, say, the 'northern euro' would have incentives to ensure that the criteria devised permitted its membership.

The second, which applies particularly to the 'southern euro', is whether the two groupings would be sufficiently coherent to overcome the divergence issues of the euro itself. The differences in institutional arrangements could be significantly smaller for a 'northern euro' than within the eurozone, but would still remain. The institutional differences for a 'southern euro' would remain substantial. Likewise, the differences in economic performance with regard to the current account would be lessened (depending on which countries are included where).

The third raises the question of the policy framework governing each of the euros. Many of those problems come from 'design faults' of the euro: the 'one size fits all' problem of monetary policy, the fiscal consolidation mentality in a context of differing needs, and the lack of a federal budget. The position of the central banks associated with each of the two 'euros' could well face the issues which the ECB faces, specifically the 'one size fits all' problem of setting a common policy suitable for a set of diverse economies. Adopting a policy framework similar to the present one would mean that the problems of the present framework continue. The only significant change would appear to be that the exchange rate between the 'northern euro' and the 'southern euro' would depart from 1:1 and could vary over time.

The fourth concerns the relationships between the 'northern euro' and the 'southern euro'. It would seem that the exchange rate between the 'northern euro' and 'southern euro' would be market determined and that, at least initially, it would be expected that the 'southern euro' would depreciate against the 'northern euro'.

Concluding comments

The aim of the so-called Five Presidents' Report, *Completing Europe's Economic and Monetary Union* (European Commission 2015), is by the year 2025, to gradually achieve 'a genuine economic and monetary union', which would gradually evolve towards 'economic, financial and fiscal union'. A preceding report (European Council 2012, the Four Presidents' Report) had proposed closer integration in four main areas: banking union; closer integration of budgetary policies; better coordination of economic policies *other* than fiscal policy; and a strengthening of democratic legitimation and accountability. The banking union has been worked on as indicated just above. The 2015 proposals contain two consecutive stages: the first stage (1 July 2015–30 June 2017) 'would build on existing instruments and make the best possible use of the existing Treaties' (European Commission 2015: 5). In the second stage (mid-2017 to 2025), 'concrete measures of a more far-reaching nature would be agreed to complete the EMU's economic and institutional architecture' (European Commission 2015: 5).

These proposals do not address the austerity framework of fiscal policy and continue to emphasize 'fiscal discipline'. It is also suggested that the creation of a European Fiscal Board to carry out independent checks on the conduct of fiscal policy is important. However, this proposal 'should not be conceived as a way to equalize incomes between Member States' (European Commission 2015: 15).

'The Stability and Growth Pact remains the anchor for fiscal stability and confidence in the respect of our fiscal rules' (European Commission 2015: 18). What would be responsible would be to use fiscal policy to achieve a high level of employment (how high has to depend on the productive capacity of the economy). The Five Presidents' Report recognizes that 'It is important to ensure also that the sum of national budget balances leads to an appropriate fiscal stance at the level of the euro area as a whole' (European Commission 2015: 14). And then '[t]here are many ways for a currency union to progress towards a Fiscal Union. Yet, while the degree to which currency unions have common budgetary instruments differs, all mature Monetary Unions have put in place a common macroeconomic stabilisation function to better deal with shocks that cannot be managed at the national level alone' (European Commission 2015: 14).

Stiglitz (2016) argues that 'the halfway house in which Europe finds itself is unsustainable: there either has to be "more Europe" or "less"; there has to be either more economic and political integration or a dissolution of the eurozone in its current form.' In this chapter, some proposals for a 'more Europe' approach to the problems of the euro area have been advanced. These proposals combine

'more Europe' with shifts in macroeconomic policies in a more progressive direction. Now the severe
obstacles which the adoption of anything like those
proposals would face have to be confronted.

5

Barriers to Progress

Introduction

The policy agenda set out in the previous chapter would be a very ambitious one, to say the least. The intention of that agenda is to suggest a direction of travel which would begin to address the euro-area crises. The central argument is that moves in the direction indicated are needed to address the problems besetting the euro area – and combine adopting a more Keynesian approach to economic policy with a shift in the direction of closer political union. Therein lie the obstacles, perhaps insurmountable: the need for a paradigm shift in economic policy and the need for elements of political union.

There are (at least) three sets of major obstacles which would stand in the way of alternative policies for the euro area being developed and implemented.

The first set is what are termed ideological, arising from the dominance of neo-liberalism and ordo-liberalism in euro-area policy agenda. The second set comes from the diversity of institutional and economic structures and the ways in which they influence economic performance and policies, and the third from the political resistance to 'ever closer union'.

Ideological barriers

Neo-liberal agenda

The euro area (and more generally the EMU) has a clear set of monetary and fiscal policy arrangements as set out in the Stability and Growth Pact and in the fiscal compact, even though in practice the policies are not fully adhered to, notably in respect of budget deficits (which have to some degree softened the austerity measures which would have otherwise been followed). The advocacy of economic policy arrangements is to be understood by reference to a particular macroeconomic analysis – in the case of the macroeconomic policies of the euro area, by reference to what is now known as the 'new consensus macroeconomics'.[1] Any specific macroeconomic analysis puts forward a view of how the economy operates, what are the issues that policy can and should address, and what would be the effectiveness (or otherwise) of particular policies, and the new consensus macroeconomics is no exception. The 'new consensus in macroeconomics' portrays an economy as essentially stable, with fiscal policy ineffectual, and focuses on interest-rate policy to control inflation without any need to address issues of financial instability.

The current policy agenda is neo-liberal in the sense that there is an underlying assumption about the efficiency of markets and their ability to secure macroeconomic stability and high levels of employment. The operation of markets, and particularly labour markets, is viewed as inherently stable, based around supply-side determined levels of output and employment which in the 'new consensus in macroeconomics' are represented by 'potential output' and the non-accelerating inflation rate of unemployment (NAIRU). Monetary policy is assigned the task of targeting inflation (by the use of policy interest rate) through a (politically) independent central bank, thereby elevating bankers' decision making above democratic decision making. Fiscal policy is viewed as impotent, though its role as something of an automatic stabilizer is recognized. Although it does not feature prominently in the 'new consensus in macroeconomics', employment (and hence unemployment) and output are very dependent on the structures of labour and product markets in the belief that liberalized and unregulated markets are conducive to low levels of unemployment and high levels of output. It is such beliefs in the benefits of liberalized markets that have underpinned the calls for 'structural reforms'. The macroeconomic policies of the EMU which have been discussed clearly fit this neo-liberal agenda.

The view that the European Union and its policy stances are neo-liberal has long been contested, and ideas of a European social model and a 'social Europe' can be counterpoised to the pursuit of a neo-liberal agenda. However, the promotion of 'structural reforms' within the EMU represents a significant shift of policy agenda in a neo-liberal direction. Also, it is in its focus on macroeconomic policies that the neo-liberal agenda is much more evident.

Ordo-liberalism

The role of ordo-liberalism in the formulation of the current euro-area policy agenda is particularly important. The constraints imposed by the ordo-liberal agenda are threefold. The first is the specific policy framework which, with respect to macroeconomic policy, fits well with the neo-liberal agenda just discussed. The second is that ordo-liberalism promotes the role of law in respect of the formulation and constraints on economic policies (discussed below). The third is that ordo-liberalism is a doctrine closely related to Germany and its macroeconomic policies, with many aspects of that doctrine having wide political acceptance in Germany (Young 2014). It is acknowledged that there are different branches of ordo-liberalism (Young 2015), and the intention here is to sum-marize the broad thrusts of ordo-liberalism and the ways in which it serves to constrain policy reformu-lation within the EMU.

Dullien and Guérot (2012) outline some of the essential features of German ordo-liberalism which include a focus on price stability, central bank independence, state–market relationships and regu-latory state intervention in markets, which they contrast with the 'position more predominant in Anglo-Saxon debate and in international institu-tions'. They continue by saying that ordo-liberalism places a greater emphasis on preventing cartels and monopolies compared with other schools of liberal-ism and neo-liberalism. Ordo-liberalism rejects the use of expansionary fiscal and monetary policies to stabilize the business cycle in a recession and can be viewed as anti-Keynesian. In a similar vein, 'ordoliberalism distinguishes itself ... in its focus upon rules and order, and defining the government's role in terms of establishing a strict order around which the market can exist and flourish', which leads to 'notions of rigid monetary policy focused exclusively on price stability' (Aziz 2015) (and much more besides). The rules-based legalistic ordo-liberal doctrine prevents adoption of Keynesian policies to challenge austerity. The adherence to fiscal discipline in the 'fiscal compact', with the constitutional requirements for balanced budgets, the limits on debts, the role of independent central banks and adherence to price stability, clearly reflects an ordo-liberal approach (Young 2014).

The policies which are closely associated with ordo-liberalism in the field of macroeconomic policies are distinctive and increasingly anti-Keynesian. With regard to fiscal policy, the German constitution had required that the current budget be in balance, allowing borrowing for public investment purposes. These requirements, broadly speaking, applied at both the federal level and the land level. This led to a German budget position which was generally in deficit, with significant levels of public investment and a debt ratio of around 60 per cent. As many pointed out at the time of the Maastricht

Treaty, the figures in the convergence criteria of 3 per cent budget deficit to GDP ratio and 60 per cent debt to GDP ratio were rather close to the German experience. However, the 'debt brake' introduced as a change to the German constitution in 2009, with full implementation over the period 2016 to 2020, switched to the overall budget being in balance or surplus, and again applicable at the federal and the land levels. In this regard, the 'debt brake' was a clear forerunner of the 'fiscal compact' with its emphasis on a balanced structural budget and the incorporation of that requirement into national constitutions

With ordo-liberalism, economic policies are embedded into law, and even more into a constitution which limits the ability to change those policies. The major examples relevant for this book come from placing fiscal and monetary policy in a constitutional framework which thereby shifts policy from being discretionary to being constrained by mandatory rules. This is rather more than the 'rules' versus 'discretion' debates which ran through many macroeconomic policy debates. In that context, the 'rule' (e.g. Taylor's rule for monetary policy) was not embedded into law, and it was recognized that 'rules' and complete 'discretion' were two ends of the spectrum, and in practice there were always strong elements of discretion, not least related to the assessment of the economic situation (e.g. in Taylor's rule, what was the output gap? What is the expected rate of inflation?). The incorporation of rules into a constitution (or equivalent) makes them difficult to change. If the chosen rule has universal validity, this does not constitute a problem. But in the context of macroeconomic policies, the rules reflect specific forms of economic and political analysis (consider, for example, the rule of independent central banks), and the general acceptability of the underpinning analysis changes over time. While the general notion of an independent central bank was accepted in Germany in the form of the Bundesbank, it did not come into wider use until the mid-1990s. Even then, governments often have reserve powers to give instructions to the central bank (as in the United Kingdom), and the objectives given to the central bank have changed, using the UK example, from inflation targeting to also include 'financial stability'.

There are two aspects associated with ordo-liberalism which serve to place constraints on changing the policy agenda. The first is the constitutional law-based approach to economic policy, particularly with regard to fiscal and monetary policy. It has, of course, been argued that the present policy framework is wrong-headed. And also that (though not for Germany) it reflected a fashion for 'independent' central banks pursuing inflation targeting; it also limits the ability to 'update' policy, for example by incorporating financial stability as an objective of the ECB. This constitutional-law approach is reflected in the 'fiscal compact', which has been introduced into national laws that are difficult to amend.

Many of the policy arrangements of the EMU are embedded into treaty arrangements, notably the Treaty of Lisbon and the Treaty on Stability, Coordination and Governance. These treaty arrangements can have implications for those EU members that are not within the EMU, for example with regard to budget deficits, and as signatories to the Treaty on Stability. Many of the fundamental changes which have been argued to be important would likely require changes to the Treaty of Lisbon. And such changes require unanimity among member governments, and in some cases agreement through national referenda. The most significant would be to the constitutional position of the European Central Bank. There would have to be changes in the Stability and Growth Pact and in the 'fiscal compact'. But in practice the SGP has not been fully applied and

there may well be sufficient flexibility of interpretation and application to enable relaxation of
fiscal austerity.

The second aspect comes from the degree to
which some of the precepts of ordo-liberalism in
the form of monetary and fiscal policies suit some
national (notably German) interests and not others.
Germany has often been seen as pursuing a neo-
mercantilist agenda in which the achievement of a
significant export surplus is strongly desired. It is
evident from its larger export surplus that Germany
is in a strong export position. It may well have
been aided in this by its membership of the euro in
so far as the exchange rate of the euro against the
dollar tends to be lower than what would have been
the equivalent exchange rate of the Deutschmark
against the dollar. Further, as indicated in chapter
2, German prices have tended to fall relative to the
prices of the other euro-area members. The export
surplus which Germany has achieved makes the
achievement of a government budget in surplus
easier – as can be seen by reference to equation (1)
in chapter 2. In broad terms, Germany has high net
private savings (savings considerably in excess of
private domestic investment) which are lent overseas (the counterpart of the export surplus), leaving
the budget approximately in balance.

The pursuit of neo-mercantilism is not directly related to ordo-liberalism. It does, however, reinforce some of the precepts of ordo-liberalism. Germany has been successful in meeting the budget requirements aided by its strong net export position – prompting an 'if we can do it, why can't you?' mentality.[2] Further, the perceived improvement in German competitiveness has been attributed to the path of real wages and the declining wage share, which may also be associated with the implementation of the Hartz labour-market reforms in the mid-2000s.

Institutional constraints

Countries came to the monetary union (and the EU more generally) with different histories, different political discourses and different institutional arrangements. In the formation of a free-trading arrangement, differences between countries are a source of mutual gain when they relate to comparative advantage between countries. The greater the differences, the more opportunity for beneficial trade to develop. In the formation of a currency union, differences between member countries in terms of their histories, policy perspectives and economic structures can pose obstacles. For the euro area, this can be seen, for example, in the ways in which trade relations between the euro area and the rest of the world and the exchange rate of the euro have differing effects across countries. The inevitable 'one size fits all' aspects of monetary policy means that the policy interest rate set by the central bank will have differential effects across countries, and the impact on the rate of inflation (the objective of monetary policy) will be more or less effective.

From the perspective of a currency union, how much do institutional differences matter, and how much do they impede the successful operation of a single currency? The 'varieties of capitalism' literature provides a strong argument that there are major differences in institutional arrangements and policy approaches between market capitalist economies, which concern the institutions of the labour markets, and of product markets and financial markets. Amable (2003), for example, provides a five-way classification, of which the first four are relevant to the EMU: market-based continental European capitalism, social democratic economics, Southern European capitalism and Asian capitalism.

It has long been argued that differences in institutional arrangements in labour markets and in respect of wage determination can create difficulties in the context of a single currency which requires broadly similar rates of price inflation and wage inflation relative to productivity. Different institutional arrangements involve different inflationary tendencies and differences in the ways in which wages and prices respond to changes in demand.

The continuation of a single currency requires similarities of inflation rates across the constituent countries and regions: yet there have been continuing differences between inflation rates. The wage- and price-setting arrangements in a country have strongly impacted upon inflationary tendencies and on how, for example, inflationary conditions respond to policy initiatives designed to address inflation – specifically the effects of interest rates in an inflation-targeting policy environment. There are two alternative responses to this: a 'cross your fingers' approach that there will be convergence between the inflationary mechanisms and that wage and price setters in each country will somehow realize that a uniformity of price inflation will need to be achieved and act accordingly; or an attempt to put in place coordination mechanisms which will aid the convergence of inflation.

A major difference between member countries, to which attention has already been drawn, relates to their industrial structures as reflected in their export potentials and import requirements. This means, for example, that countries have different interests with regard to the euro rate of exchange (e.g. relative to the dollar). More significantly, current account imbalances impose constraints on growth rates. And the differences in sectoral positions have requirements for different budget positions. Thus the macroeconomic policies must pay regard to those differences since seeking to impose common fiscal policies on diverse situations is a recipe for trouble.

Developing institutional and policy arrangements to apply across all of the member countries, which in effect operate at the federal level, always runs into the issue of the diversity of existing such arrangements. Two examples can be given. The first relates to the development of a federal-level unemployment insurance scheme which would have to allow for current differences between countries with respect to the scale and composition of unemployment benefits and the degree to which the income of the unemployed comes from insurance schemes (rather than, say, means-tested social assistance). A second example would be any development of a common corporation profits tax from the current position where the rate of tax varies between countries, with some using low tax rates as a policy instrument. Other relevant differences are the way profits are calculated, what allowances there are against tax and the relative importance of corporations. This is not to argue that such policies would become impossible but rather that there would likely be winners and losers involved in a common policy more in tune with some countries than with others.

In the context of the EMU, particularly with its insistence on common budget obligations, the configuration of sectoral balances is significant. One representation of this is the identification of 'three types of regimes under the conditions of financialization, namely a debt-led private demand boom, an export-led mercantilist and a domestic demand-led regime' (Dodig, Hein and Detzer 2015). These authors relate these different regimes to different forms of instability and the generation of financial crisis. Of particular significance here is that each of the regimes can be unsustainable in different ways, reflect different policy outlooks and have implications for the appropriate budget position. Germany has been viewed as the key player in the pursuit of a neo-mercantilist export surplus approach (Sawyer 2014), though it would not be alone among EMU members in that. One clear aspect of the widening current account imbalances among EMU countries prior to the financial crisis was the ballooning export surpluses of some northern European countries.

These brief remarks on differences between countries are made to raise the following issues and to indicate some of the difficulties which the construction of policy alternatives faces. The first is how close in institutional structure, economic policy outlook and industrial structure countries need to be in order for a currency union to operate effectively. It can be argued that countries need to be sufficiently close that, for example, there are similar generating processes for inflation and that the use of policy instruments to constrain inflation have similar effects.

The second issue is the difficulties which differing institutional arrangements pose for the construction of union-wide policies. The 'one size fits all' problems of monetary policy have been well rehearsed. The SGP and the 'fiscal compact' have sought to impose a single budget policy on economies with different structures. The construction of a banking union has to cope with different banking structures.

When the euro was being formulated, hopes were often expressed that the single currency, along with the single market, would bring convergence of economic circumstances and institutional arrangements, thereby enhancing the performance of the single currency and its associated economies. Such convergence has not occurred on any large scale, and hence the difficulties of applying policies across diverse economies remain. Ferreiro et al. (2016) have shown that, since the creation of the EMU, the structural differences between the euro countries have not declined but are even larger, a divergence process that increased during the current great recession. There has not been the real convergence between the euro-area countries that had been hoped for, and policies to achieve convergence are now required.

Political resistance

Many have long argued, as indicated above, that for a currency union to be sustainable over decades, it will need to be embedded in political union. The type of proposals in the previous chapter represent elements of moves towards some key features of political union, notably the adoption of an EU/EMU fiscal policy and its own taxation. In that respect, those proposals should be seen as a recognition that forms of political union are necessary for the sustainable prosperity of the euro area. Other policy proposals require further integration and coordination of policies: the development of a banking union clearly fits into that category.

There would be very substantial and perhaps insurmountable obstacles, which may be termed 'political', to the adoption and implementation of policies along the lines envisaged. These political obstacles and constraints are discussed under three headings.

First, moves to some form of fiscal union involve fiscal transfers between nations and regions. Under a progressive tax and expenditure system, implicitly or explicitly, poorer regions and countries would gain and richer regions and countries lose. Federal currency unions, such as the United States, Australia and Canada, do involve substantial transfers between the constituent states and provinces both indirectly, through the operation of federal tax policies with higher revenues being raised in more prosperous regions, and directly, through grants to less prosperous regions. Proposals to enhance regional and structural funds within the EU would similarly involve favouring less prosperous regions at the expense of the more prosperous.

The significance of some form of fiscal union has been stated in the following way:

in the long run the monetary union will have to be embedded in a significant fiscal union. This is probably the hardest part of the process to make the Eurozone sustainable in the long run, as the willingness to transfer significant spending and taxing powers to European institutions is very limited. It remains a necessary part, though. Without significant steps towards fiscal union there is no future for the euro. (De Grauwe 2013: 31)

It is easy to envisage the political resistance to the development of elements of a fiscal union with its combination of an enhanced EU budget and fiscal transfers between the regions and nations involved.

Second, in the present more nationalistic climate in many European countries, the prospect of power and decisions shifting towards the European Commission and the Council of Ministers is unlikely to be received favourably in many quarters (to put it mildly). Around one-third of the MEPs elected in the European Parliamentary election of 2014 are eurosceptic, belonging to a range of parliamentary groupings and parties, such as Europe of Freedom and Direct Democracy and Europe of Nations and Freedom. These parties generally combine anti-immigrant/anti-Muslim policies with euroscepticism, pushing for withdrawal from the euro and/or from the European Union. In the past few years, there has been a rise in vote share and influence on the political debate of what are often termed populist, nationalistic and anti-immigrant parties, for example, the Front National in France, the AdD in Germany and the Freedom Party (PVV), led by Geert Wilders in the Netherlands. In Italy, the Five-Star Movement, at the time of writing scoring over 30 per cent in opinion polls, promotes a referendum on euro membership and campaigns for Italy to leave. These nationalistic and dis-integrationist forces threaten any developments towards further cooperation and integration across the EU. In voting terms, the nationalistic so-called populist parties remain a minority, the only electoral victory to date being the referendum vote in the United Kingdom to leave the EU.

There does, however, remain general support for the euro within the euro area, running at 70% in favour, 25% against, though in 2016 outside the euro area it ran at 33% to 59%, indicating a lack of enthusiasm in those countries for joining the euro (European Commission 2016). Does support such as that (and the degree of enthusiasm from those in favour of the euro cannot be gleaned from such statistics, nor how much concern there is over the consequences for a country of leaving the euro) provide sufficient political impetus for the further political integration and policy changes which are required to enable the euro area to prosper?

In a White Paper of March 2017, the European Commission considered five scenarios for the EU to 2025 ('carrying on'; 'nothing but the single market'; 'those who want more, do more'; 'doing less more efficiently'; 'doing much more together'). The European Commission (2017: 6) acknowledges that 'many Europeans consider the Union as either too distant or too interfering in their day-to-day lives. Others question its added-value and ask how Europe improves their standard of living. And for too many, the EU fell short of their expectations as it struggled with its worst financial, economic and social crisis in post-war history.' High levels of youth unemployment and slow or negative growth were viewed as having:

> fuelled doubts about the EU's social market economy and its ability to deliver on its promise to leave no one behind and to ensure that every generation is better off than the previous one. This has been particularly felt within the euro area, highlighting the need to complete the Economic and Monetary Union and strengthen the convergence of economic and social performances. Making Europe's

economy more inclusive, competitive, resilient and future-proof will be no less demanding in the years ahead. (European Commission 2017: 9)

However, the role of the formation of the euro and the austerity nature of its macroeconomic policies have clearly contributed to the high levels of unemployment and slow growth. The proposals sketched in the previous chapter would themselves contribute to the completion of the EMU and to convergence of economic performance. But they would do so through taking economic policies in a different direction from the present neo-liberal one, and they would present much greater possibilities for addressing unemployment and raising prosperity.

Third, the policy changes would have to be agreed by the member states and the European Parliament. Some of the changes that are akin to extensions to existing policies may only require a qualified majority vote. Others would require unanimity among the member states and in some cases involve amending the Treaty of Lisbon (with its two parts, the Treaty on European Union and the Treaty on the Functioning of the European Union). Revising the 'independence' and the policy objectives of the ECB would be a major adjustment requiring treaty change (and, as indicated above, would challenge the ordo-liberal orthodoxy). The 'fiscal compact' imposition of a balance in each country's structural budget has been written into national constitutions or equivalent: as argued above, this policy is detrimental and probably unachievable and in need of revision. Reinterpretation of the 'fiscal compact' (e.g. redefining what is understood by a structural budget and working in terms of the current budget position to allow borrowing for capital investment) could ease its austerity. Where there is the political will to do so, the legal obstacles could in some cases be circumvented. But it remains the case that some countries would face severe constraints in making the required changes.

Concluding comments

The euro area is to be regarded as more of a 'pessimal currency area' than an 'optimal currency area'. With sufficient political effort, the eurozone may well be able to stagger on for many years to come. It may also be locked into present arrangements because of the enormous difficulties of making the changes to disassemble the single currency. It is rather like being at the bottom of a valley with water flowing through it which is threatening to engulf those in the valley, but on both sides of the valley the terrain and incline preclude being able to scramble out.

The policy agenda advanced in the previous chapter to address the euro-area crises and to restore prosperity to the euro area faces formidable obstacles to its implementation. The political forces which could shift economic policies in the directions suggested are weak or non-existent. The policy agenda requires a sharp break with the neoliberal macroeconomic agenda which has become so embedded in the policy thinking and arrangements of the euro area. There are severe constraints put on change by the ways in which the nature of macroeconomic policies and economic institutions are situated in treaties which require unanimity across member states to change. The proposed policy agenda would also represent recognition that a currency union needs to be underpinned by a degree of political union if it is to be sustained. At a time when there is much more focus on the possibilities of disintegration rather than of integration, conditions are not propitious for developing further economic amalgamation. Yet, unless profound reforms are made, the euro area, and more importantly the people of the European Union, face an uncomfortable future.

Notes

1 Throughout the book, the terminology used will be that of the euro area and its policies. The countries of the European Union are members of the Economic and Monetary Union (EMU), with 19 out of (at present) 28 EU members having adopted the euro. Many of the policies, particularly in respect of budget deficits, apply to all the countries of the EMU. As our discussion focuses on the euro (and in particular the consequences of fixed exchange rates between euro adopters), I will refer to the euro area and its economic policies.

2 Eleven countries (Austria, Belgium, Finland, France, Germany, Ireland, Italy, Luxembourg, the Netherlands, Portugal and Spain) were accepted for membership in 1998, joined by Greece in 2001. Subsequent members have been Cyprus (2008), Estonia (2011), Latvia (2011), Lithuania (2015), Malta (2008), Slovakia (2009) and Slovenia (2007).

3 https://europa.eu/european-union/about-eu/money/ euro_en.
4 See Arestis and Sawyer (2013b): ch. 2.
5 Kabderian Dreyer and Schmid (2016), for example, find that while there is a positive effect of EU membership on economic growth, there is no impact on growth in being part of the euro area, except for a negative effect during the financial crisis.
6 For some early doubts by the present author, see Arestis and Sawyer (1994, 1996).

Chapter 2 The Shaky Foundations of the Euro Project

1 Formal title: Committee for the Study of Economic and Monetary Union (chair: Jacques Delors) 1989.
2 See Arestis, Brown and Sawyer (2001): ch. 3 and specifically Table 3.1.
3 The optimal currency area (OCA) literature starts with Mundell (1961), McKinnon (1963) and Kenen (1969): for reviews, see, for example, Baldwin and Wyplosz (2009: ch. 11).
4 Information taken from Arestis, Ferrari, de Paula and Sawyer (2003), Table 1, itself based on the *Financial Times* (23 March 1999).
5 See, for example, Arestis and Sawyer (2013a).
6 Resolution of the European Council on the Stability and Growth Pact, Amsterdam, 17 June 1997.
7 The budget position involves more austerity than may appear. A zero budget deficit as recorded would be a surplus of around 1% of GDP in real terms (the fall in the value of the public debt due to inflation is

equivalent to 1.2% of GDP for a 2% rate of inflation and a 60% debt to GDP ratio).

8 I discuss this point in much more detail in Sawyer (2012).

Chapter 3 The Failures of the Euro Area

1 See, for example, Ferreiro and Gómez (2017) for supporting evidence with regard to employment and unemployment in Europe in the past decade.

2 This is repeated in almost every issue of the *Monthly Bulletin* of the ECB; see also, for example, the governor of the ECB, Mario Draghi (2013).

3 See, for example, Arestis and Sawyer (2013b): ch. 6.

4 Figures taken from OECD *Economic Outlook*, June 2016.

5 See Sawyer (2012, 2015) for more detailed and technical discussion.

6 These figures are taken from OECD *Economic Outlook*, May 2009 and May 2011, respectively.

7 See, for example, the web pages http://www.levyinsti tute.org/topics/greek-economic-crisis for publications over the past seven years covering the evolving Greek crises and proposals for alleviation; also see Karyotis and Gedrodimos (2015) for many papers on the Greek crisis and time line of the crisis.

8 The Memorandum of Understanding (2015) between the troika and the Greek government sets out clearly what those 'structural reforms' entail. As it was put in the letter from then Greek prime minister George

Papandreou, agreeing to the MOU, 'despite the fact that we support Collective Bargaining and Agreements between social partners on principle (a longstanding European value and position recently included in the proposed new Treaty changes), our Party [PASOK] has decided and supports the deep structural reforms in the labor, product and service markets. The agreed adjustment of labor market parameters has been taken in order to give a strong upfront impetus to unit labor-cost reductions, and promote employment and economic activity.'

9 See, for example, Rodriguez and Carrasco (2014), Arestis (2015), Dodig and Herr (2015) and FESSUD (2017) for elaborations and critiques of the policies pursued by the ECB after the financial crisis.

Chapter 4 *An Agenda for Prosperity*

1 The policy agenda which is now outlined draws on Arestis, McCauley and Sawyer (2001) where an alternative Stability and Growth Pact was proposed (Sawyer 2012, 2016) and influenced by papers such as that by Hein and Detzer (2015). The annual publication of the Euromemo by the Euromemorandum Group contains alternative progressive policy agendas (available at http://www.euromemo.eu/euromemo randum/index.html). Rosa-Luxemburg-Stiftung and Policy Research in Macroeconomics (2017), published after this manuscript was completed, brings forward policies consistent with those here, applied more generally to the future of the European Union.

2 See https://ec.europa.eu/priorities/jobs-growth-and-investment/investment-plan_en for ongoing information on the plan; and http://bruegel.org/2016/05/assessing-the-juncker-plan-after-one-year/ for assessment of the first year of operation.

3 See https://ec.europa.eu/info/strategy/european-semester/framework/europe-2020-strategy_en for Europe 2020 strategy as seen by the European Commission.

4 See, for example, a forum on 'Designing a European Unemployment Insurance Scheme', *Intereconomics* 49(4) (July 2014): 184–203, contributions by Andor, Dullien, Jara and Sutherland; see also Beblavý, Marconi and Maselli (2015) and Spath (2015).

Chapter 5 Barriers to Progress

1 Arestis (2007) contains a range of papers on the 'new consensus in macroeconomics'. For a critique, see Arestis (2009). In its more elaborated forms, dynamic stochastic general equilibrium (DSGE) models, it has become the standard approach to economic modelling within central banks and elsewhere (for discussion in relation to the Bank of England, see Arestis and Sawyer 2002).

2 Paetz, Rietzler and Truger (2016) remark that 'one might be forgiven for thinking that the federal government debt brake has been a great success. The net borrowing rules have been consistently over-fulfilled, extremely rapid budget consolidation has occurred since 2010 and the debt brake model has been copied at European level in the shape of the European Fiscal

Compact. But appearances can be deceptive' (p. 1). They ascribed the move of the budget into surplus to positive employment and income growth and low interest rates.

References

Aiginger, K. (2016) 'A strategy change for Europe: Old myths versus new roads'. *Intereconomics* 2016(1): 28–33.

Almunia, J. (2008) 'Foreword', in European Commission, 'EMU@10: Successes and challenges after ten years of Economic and Monetary Union'. *European Economy* 2.

Amable, B. (2003) *The Diversity of Modern Capitalism.* Oxford: Oxford University Press.

Andor, L. (2014) 'Basic European unemployment insurance – the best way forward in strengthening the EMU's resilience and Europe's recovery'. *Intereconomics* 49(4): 184–9.

Arestis, P. (ed.) (2007) *Is There a New Consensus in Macroeconomics?* Basingstoke: Palgrave Macmillan.

Arestis, P. (2009) 'New consensus macroeconomics: A critical appraisal', in E. Hein, T. Niechoj and E. Stockhammer (eds), *Macroeconomic Policies on*

References

Shaky Foundations – Whither Mainstream Economics?
Marburg: Metropolis Verlag.

Arestis, P. (2015) 'Current and future ECB monetary policy'. *Brazilian Keynesian Review* 1(1): 4–17.

Arestis, P. and Sawyer, M. (1994) 'Making the "euro" palatable'. *New Economy* 3: 89–91.

Arestis, P. and Sawyer, M. (1996) 'Unemployment and the independent European system of central banks: Prospects and some alternative arrangements'. *American Journal of Economics and Sociology* 56(3): 353–68.

Arestis, P. and Sawyer, M. (2002) 'The Bank of England macroeconomic model: Its nature and implications'. *Journal of Post Keynesian Economics* 24(2): 529–46.

Arestis, P. and Sawyer, M. (2008) 'New consensus macroeconomics and inflation targeting: Keynesian critique'. *Economia e Sociedade*, Campinas, 17, special edn, pp. 629–54.

Arestis, P. and Sawyer, M. (2011) 'The design faults of the Economic and Monetary Union'. *Journal of Contemporary European Studies* 19(1): 19–30.

Arestis, P. and Sawyer, M. (2013a) 'Must we move to a United States of Europe?' *Challenge* 56(3): 42–52.

Arestis, P. and Sawyer, M. (2013b) *Economic and Monetary Union Macroeconomic Policies: Current Practices and Alternatives*. Basingstoke: Palgrave Macmillan.

Arestis, P., Brown, A. and Sawyer, M. (2001) *The*

References

Euro: Evolution and Prospects. Cheltenham: Edward Elgar.

Arestis, P., Ferrari, F., de Paula, L. Z. and Sawyer, M. (2003) 'The euro and the EMU: Lessons for Mercosur', in P. Arestis and L. Fernanando de Paula (eds), *Monetary Union in South America: Lessons from EMU*. Cheltenham: Edward Elgar.

Arestis, P., McCauley, K. and Sawyer, M. (2001) 'An alternative stability pact for the European Union'. *Cambridge Journal of Economics* 25(1): 113–30.

Aziz, J. (2015) *The Trouble with Ordoliberalism*, http://www.pieria.co.uk/articles/the_trouble_with_ordoliberalism

Baldwin, R. E. and Wyplosz, C. (2009) *The Economics of European Integration*. Maidenhead: McGraw-Hill Higher Education.

Beblavý, M., Marconi, G. and Maselli, I. (2015) 'A European unemployment benefits scheme: The rationale and the challenges ahead'. *EPS Special Report* 119 (September).

Capaldo, J. and Izurieta, A. (2013) 'The imprudence of labour market flexibilization in a fiscally austere world'. *International Labour Review* 152(1): 1–26.

Committee for the Study of Economic and Monetary Union (chair Jacques Delors) (1989) *Report on Economic and Monetary Union in the European Community*, http://aei.pitt.edu/1007/1/monetary_delors.pdf

Coudert, V., Couharde, C. and Mignon, V. (2013) 'On

References

currency misalignments within the euro area'. *Review of International Economics* 21(1): 35–48.

De Grauwe, P. (2013) 'Design failures in the eurozone: Can they be fixed?' LSE 'Europe in Question' Discussion Paper Series (LEQS) No. 57, February.

De Grauwe, P. (2015) 'Design failures of the Eurozone', 7 September, http://voxeu.org/article/design-failures-eurozone

Dodig, N. and Herr, H. (2015) 'EU policies addressing current account imbalances in the EMU: An assessment', *FESSUD Working Paper Series*, No. 74.

Dodig, N., Hein, E. and Detzer, D. (2015) 'Financialisation and the financial and economic crisis: Theoretical framework and empirical analysis for 15 countries'. *FESSUD Working Paper Series*, No. 110.

Draghi, M. (2012) 'Speech by Mario Draghi, President of the European Central Bank' at the Global Investment Conference, London, 26 July, http://www.ecb.europa.eu/press/key/date/2012/html/sp120726.en.html

Draghi, M. (2013) 'Introductory statement to the press conference'. European Central Bank, 4 April.

Dreyer, J. K. and Schmid, P. A. (2016) 'Growth effects of EU and EZ memberships: Empirical findings from the first 15 years of the Euro'. *Journal of Economic Modelling*. http://dx.doi.org/10.1016/j.econmod.2016.09.007

Dullien, S. and Guérot, U. (2012) *The Long Shadow of Ordoliberalism: Germany's Approach to the Euro*

References

Crisis. Policy Brief. London: European Council on Foreign Relations.

European Commission (MacDougall Report) (1977) *Report of the Study Group on the Role of Public Finance in European Integration*. Brussels: European Commission.

European Commission (2008) 'EMU@10: Successes and challenges after ten years of Economic and Monetary Union'. *European Economy* 2. Luxembourg: Publications of the European Union.

European Commission (2010) 'Surveillance of Intra-Euro-Area: Competitiveness and Imbalances'. *European Economy* 1. Luxembourg: Publications of the European Union.

European Commission (2015) *Completing Europe's Economic and Monetary Union*. Report by J.-C. Juncker, in close cooperation with D. Tusk, J. Dijsselbloem, M. Draghi and M. Schulz. Brussels, 22 June.

European Commission (2016) *Standard Eurobarometer 86: Public Opinion in the European Union: First Results*. Luxembourg: Publications of the European Union.

European Commission (2017) 'White Paper on the Future of Europe: Reflections and Scenarios for the EU27 by 2025'. https://ec.europa.eu/commission/sites/beta-political/files/white_paper_on_the_future_of_europe_en.pdf

European Council (2012) *Towards a Genuine Economic*

References

and Monetary Union. Report by H. van Rompuy, in close collaboration with J. M. Barroso, J.-C. Juncker and M. Draghi, 5 December.

European Union (2012) *Treaty on Stability, Coordination and Governance in the Economic and Monetary Union*. Brussels: European Union.

Ferreiro, J. and Gómez, C. (forthcoming) 'The great recession and the labour markets in Europe: Do labour institutions matter?' in P. Arestis and M. Sawyer (eds), *Economic Policies since the Global Financial Crisis*. Basingstoke: Palgrave Macmillan.

Ferreiro, J., Gálvez, C., Gómez, C. and González, A. (2016) 'The impact of the Great Recession on the European Union countries'. *FESSUD Working Paper Series*, No. 150.

FESSUD (2017) 'Financialisation Economy Society and Sustainable Development', *FESSUD Working Paper Series*, No. 206.

Godley, W. (1992) 'Maastricht and all that'. *London Review of Books* 14(19), 8 October, pp. 3–4, http://www.lrb.co.uk/v14/n19/wynne-godley/maastricht-and-all-that

Hein, E. and Detzer, D. (2015) 'Coping with imbalances in the Euro area: Policy alternatives addressing divergences and disparities between member countries'. *FESSUD Working Paper Series*, No. 63.

Hermann, C. (2014) 'Structural adjustment and neo-liberal convergence in labour markets and welfare: The impact of the crisis and austerity measures on

References

European economic and social models'. *Competition and Change* 18(2) (April): 111–30.

Jarocinski, M. and Lenza, M. (2016) 'How large is the output gap in the euro area', https://www.ecb.europa.eu/pub/economic-research/resbull/2016/html/rb160701.en.html

Karyotis, G. and Gerodimos, R. (eds) (2015) *The Politics of Extreme Austerity: Greece in the Eurozone Crisis*. London: AIAA.

Kenen, P. (1969) 'The theory of optimum currency areas: an eclectic view', in R. A. Mundell and A. K. Swoboda (eds), *Monetary Problems of the International Economy*. Chicago and London: University of Chicago Press, pp. 59–77.

Landesmann, M. (2015) 'Industrial policy: Its role in the European economy'. *Intereconomics* 50(3): 133–8.

Lavoie, M. and Stockhammer, E. (eds) (2013) *Wage-led Growth: An Equitable Strategy for Economic Recovery*. Basingstoke: Palgrave Macmillan and Geneva: International Labour Office.

Marjolin, R. (1975) *Report of the Study Group 'Economic and Monetary Union 1980' and Annex I. 8 March 1975* (commonly called the Marjolin Report) [EU Commission Working Document].

Marsh, D. (2011) *The Euro: The Battle for the New Global Currency*. New Haven and London: Yale University Press.

Marsh, D. (2013) *Europe's Deadlock: How the Euro*

References

Crisis could be Solved – and Why It Won't Happen.
New Haven and London: Yale University Press.

Mazier, J. and Petit, P. (2013) 'In search of sustainable paths for the eurozone in the troubled post-2008 world'. *Cambridge Journal of Economics* 37: 513–32.

Mazzucato, M., Cimoli, M., Dosi, G. et al. (2015) 'Which industrial policy does Europe need?' *Intereconomics* 50(3): 120–55.

McKinnon, R. I. (1963) 'Optimum currency areas'. *American Economic Review* 53: 717–25.

Memorandum of Understanding (2015) *Memorandum of Understanding between the European Commission Acting on behalf of the European Stability Mechanism and the Hellenic Republic and the Bank of Greece*, August 2015, http://ec.europa.eu/economy_finance/ assistance_eu_ms/greek_loan_facility/pdf/01_mou_ 20150811_en.pdf

Mundell, R. A. (1961) 'A theory of optimum currency areas'. *American Economic Review* 51: 657–65.

Paetz, C., Rietzler, K. and Truger, A. (2016) 'The federal budget debt brake since 2011: The real test is yet to come'. *IMK Report* 117e, September.

Pianta, M. (2016) 'Why Europe needs a public investment plan'. *Intereconomics* 51(6): 312–17.

Pianta, M., Lucchese, M. and Nascia, L. (2016) 'What is to be produced? The making of a new industrial policy in Europe'. Rosa Luxemburg Stiftung, Brussels.

Rodriguez C. and Carrasco, C. (2014) 'ECB policy

responses between 2007 and 2014: A chronological analysis and a money quantity assessment of their effects'. *FESSUD Working Paper Series*, No. 65.

Rosa-Luxemburg-Stiftung and Policy Research in Macroeconomics (2017) *Bringing Democratic Choice to Europe's Economic Governance: The EU Treaty Changes We Need, and Why We Need Them*. Brussels: Rosa-Luxemburg-Stiftung.

Sawyer, M. (2012) 'The contradictions of balanced structural government budget', in H. Herr, T. Niechoj, C. Thomasberger, A. Truger and T. van Treeck (eds), *From Crisis to Growth? The Challenge of Imbalances and Debt*. Marburg: Metropolis Verlag.

Sawyer, M. (2014) 'Neo-mercantilism, inequality, financialisation and the euro crises'. *FESSUD Working Paper Series*, No. 27.

Sawyer, M. (2015) 'Can prosperity return to the Economic and Monetary Union?' *Review of Keynesian Economics* 3(4) (Winter): 457–70.

Sawyer, M. (2016) 'The Economic and Monetary Union: Past and present failures and some future possibilities'. *World Economic Review* 6: 31–43.

Smith, J. (2016) 'Controlling Eurozone current account surpluses – revisit the Treaty of Rome!' http://www.primeeconomics.org/articles/xl0id2k2pcyyhv1t68cx-spfaj0lym2

Spath, N. J. (2015) 'Automatic stabilizers for the Euro area: What is on the table?' Jacques Delors Institut, Policy Paper 166.

References

Stiglitz, J. E. (2016) *The Euro and its Threat to the Future of Europe*. London: Allen Lane.

Tridico, P. (2012) 'Financial crisis and global imbalances: Its labour market origins and the aftermath'. *Cambridge Journal of Economics* 36(1): 17–42.

Werner Report (1970) 'Report to the Council and the Commission on the Realisation by Stages of Economic and Monetary Union in the Community'. *Supplement to Bulletin of the European Communities* 11.

Young, B. (2014) 'German ordoliberalism as agenda setter for the euro crisis: Myth trumps reality'. *Journal of Contemporary European Studies* 22(3): 276–87. DOI: 10.1080/14782804.2014.937408

Young, B. (2015) 'Introduction: The highjacking of German ordoliberalism'. *European Review of International Studies* 2(3): 5–14.